HOW TO RUN A  CAMPAIGN

In this Series

How to Buy & Run a Shop
How to Choose a Private School
How to Claim State Benefits
How to Do Your Own Advertising
How to Employ & Manage Staff
How to Enjoy Retirement
How to Get a Job Abroad
How to Get That Job
How to Help Your Child at School
How to Keep Business Accounts
How to Live & Work in America
How to Live & Work in Australia
How to Live & Work in Belgium
How to Lose Weight & Keep Fit
How to Master Public Speaking
How to Pass Exams Without Anxiety
How to Prepare Your Child for School
How to Raise Business Finance
How to Start a Business from Home
How to Study Abroad
How to Study & Live in Britain
How to Succeed in Teaching
How to Survive at College
How to Survive Divorce
How to Take Care of Your Heart
How to Teach Abroad
How to Use a Library
How to Write for Publication

other titles in preparation

RUN A LOCAL CAMPAIGN

Polly Bird

NO, DO CARRY ON, I LIKE A
GOOD HECKLER....

Northcote House

DEDICATION

To Jon, with love.

© 1989 by Polly Bird
Cartoons by Dai Owen

First published in 1989 by Northcote House Publishers Ltd,
Harper & Row House, Estover Road, Plymouth PL6 7PZ, United Kingdom.
Tel: Plymouth (0752) 705251. Telex: 45635. Fax: (0752) 777603.

British Library Cataloguing in Publication Data
Bird, Polly, *1950-*
    How to run a local campaign. — (How to . . . Series).
    1. Pressure groups. Organisation
    I. Title II. Series
    322.4′3

ISBN 0-7463-0539-7

Typeset by Cheshire Typesetters
Printed in Great Britain by BPCC Wheatons Ltd, Exeter

Contents

Preface

We all think we know how to exercise our democratic rights. We simply vote for our representatives in Parliament or on the local council. Having done that, our duty is fulfilled. The state of the local roads, the need for a school crossing, the threat of closure to the local hospital we leave to 'them'. We elected our representatives — they must get on with the job.

But what if those in authority have other priorities and neglect those things close to home that seem important to us? Should we just sit back and wait for something to happen?

We all know the answer to that. *Nothing* will happen. The pavements will continue to deteriorate, the hospital will be closed, the motorway will cut through local countryside.

Some people feel that it is 'not done' to argue with the decisions of those in authority whether they are officials or democratically elected representatives of the people. They feel uneasy at the thought of confronting established authority. But democracy involves everyone. It is your locality. You have a right to make your feelings known. You have a right to try to change the minds of those in power if you are convinced they are wrong. Indeed, you owe it to your community.

Times are changing. It is no longer good enough to sit back and say 'nothing I can do will be any use' or 'someone else will do it'. Don't wait for other people to make that protest. It is up to you.

To prove that anyone can organise a local campaign successfully, let me tell you about the Save Amott Road Clinic Campaign. Jeannette Aspden and I, two mothers with young children, discovered that our local child health and well-woman clinic was threatened with closure by the local health authority. We wrote letters of protest and, much to our surprise, discovered that people expected us to run a campaign. We knew nothing about campaigning but we gave ourselves a name, organised publicity, talked to the health authority and finally persuaded them that the clinic should remain open.

It took us three years, a lot of effort and the support of many people. We did things wrong and learned by trial and error what was effective and how authority operated. This book is the result of what I have learned during those three years. I hope it will show how to run a local campaign without making the mistakes that we did.

Don't say you can't do it. Anyone can run a successful local campaign. This book will tell you how to start, how to keep going, and even how to deal with your feelings when it's all over.

In the book I use the Save Amott Road Clinic Campaign as an example. I also use examples from two fictitious campaigns, Sheila and Mary's 'Save Mill Street Playground Campaign' and John's efforts to get a pelican crossing outside his local primary school, the 'Build Whytown School Crossing Movement'.

I can't guarantee that you will win, but I believe that with the help of this book you will campaign to the best effect.

Don't leave it to someone else. Start now.

ACKNOWLEDGEMENTS

For three years Jeannette Aspden and I have worked together as joint coordinators of the Save Amott Road Clinic Campaign. During that time I have had the benefit of Jeannette's advice, enthusiasm and friendship. She was also kind enough to read this book in manuscript. For that and much else, my thanks.

I thank the editors of *The Peckham & Dulwich Comet* (including *The Star*) and *The Deptford & Peckham Mercury* newspapers for permission to reproduce cuttings from those papers.

I am grateful to the Controller of Her Majesty's Stationery Office for permission to reproduce certain Crown copyright material.

My thanks to Southwark Women's Equality Unit for permission to reproduce pages from a grant application form and a model constitution. I acknowledge with gratitude their support for SARCP.

Finally, I thank my husband, Jon, for his patience and practical support while this book was being written.

Polly Bird

1
Getting Started

FIRST STEPS

Mary is talking to her friend Sheila outside the school gates. Sheila tells Mary there is a rumour that the local park playground is about to close, leaving the children nowhere to play. 'Somebody should do something', says Mary. 'There's no point in protesting until we're sure it's going to close', replies Sheila. They do nothing and a month later the playground is closed.

Does that sort of conversation sound familiar? How many times do we all say, 'Let's wait and see' when we are faced with local problems? Let's try that again.

Sheila. 'I've heard that the local playground is about to close. I phoned the council. They didn't say it was going to close, but they didn't say it would stay open either. We must do something.'

Mary. 'Yes. I'll write a letter of protest to the council today and ask our local councillor to find out what is happening. Why don't we ask other parents to write as well? Their children would be affected.'

Sheila and Mary **start a campaign.** The council changes its mind about the playground and the children can carry on playing safely.

Which scene did you prefer? The first one is the easier; the second one needs effort from you. But if your playground, school, listed building, new zebra crossing is important, it's up to you to do something about it. If you wait for someone else to act, they usually won't. The saying, 'If you want something done, do it yourself', is as true for campaigning as for any other activity.

So, if you are concerned about something, first of all ask yourself these questions:

- Do I think the problem is important?
- Will it affect other people too?
- Is there still time to do something about it?
- Will I feel bad if I do nothing about it?

- Will the quality of life in my community be affected?
- Am I prepared to work towards solving the problem?

If you answered yes to all those questions, do something now. Reading this book should help you plan and run an effective campaign.

Start now

First of all, ignore the advice of anyone who tells you to wait and see. Once something has been done officially, it's usually done for good. It's virtually impossible to reverse an official decision once that decision has been put into practice.

Your aim must be to change official thinking before the end of any consultation period, so that the final recommendation to the decision-making body is the one you, the campaigners, want. You can go on protesting after that time, but then officials can always point out that the consultation period is over and they don't have to listen to you any more.

HOW ARE DECISIONS MADE?

Bureaucracy can seem daunting, but becomes less so the more you understand how it works — who really **makes the decisions,** who makes the recommendations and who collects the facts. If you have a problem or concern you need to know who to appeal to or who to try to persuade or influence.

At a **local level,** for instance, voters elect **councillors.** These are unpaid people who give a lot of their spare time to helping the community run smoothly. They hold regular council meetings, usually at the town hall, and generally open to the public. There they decide how the local authority's money is to be spent, what building schemes can go ahead, whether schools should be amalgamated, and so on. You will find more details about how a council works in Chapter 5.

National government, on the other hand, operates on a larger scale, but in a similar way. **Members of Parliament** (MPs) are elected by us as our representatives, and laws are passed and major decisions made by the House of Commons and the House of Lords.

Of course, there are occasions when the local community is affected by decisions made by local companies, or national companies with local branches. In some cases campaigners may find themselves making their first approaches to a managing director or chairman, or even seeking to influence shareholders. But for most local campaigners the target in the first place will be the **local council.**

BEGINNING TO ACT

So, if you have a problem and are prepared to take on bureaucracy
or officialdom, what do you do next?

The telephone enquiry

The first priority is to check your facts. Don't assume that any rumour
you have heard is true — telephone whoever you think might be causing the problem and **find out**. If you are not sure who to ask, contact
your local **Citizens' Advice Bureau,** who will advise you. They may
even have a booklet with a list of council departments for you to take
away. Otherwise, telephone the **council** number in the phone book and
ask to speak to the person in charge of the problem. You may find
you are passed from person to person, but be patient until you get the
person you want. In Mary's and Sheila's case the problem was the Mill
Street Children's Playground, and that will serve as an example.

When you are put through to the right department, ask to speak to
'the person in charge of closing the Mill Street Playground'. If you get
put through to someone straightaway it probably means that your fears
are well-founded.

More probably, though, you will be put through to 'someone who
deals with playgrounds'. If they don't automatically give their name
on answering, ask who they are and what their job in the organisation
is. **Make a note** of it for future reference. Then ask your questions as
simply as possible and **note down** the answers, again for future
reference. If you are afraid you will get flustered it may help to write
down the questions first before you make the call, so that you won't
forget anything.

Sheila would need to ask:

- Is the council planning to close the Mill Street Children's Playground?

If yes, the next questions would be:

- Why is the Playground to be closed?
- Who is in charge of the closure?
- When is the closure planned to take place?
- What sort of consultation with the public will there be?

If no, she would say:

- I've heard a rumour that it will be closed. Where would this idea have come from?
- Who would be in charge of any closure?
- Would the public be consulted if there was to be a closure?
- How long would this process take?

Even if the answer is 'No, there will be no closure', or, more likely, 'Closure is just one of the many options we are considering', make careful note of the replies. At the slightest shift towards closure you can then quote their 'no closure' words back at them.

Of course, during your initial telephone call you may be asking someone to provide something. Taking a school crossing as an example, your questions could be:

- Who is in charge of providing school crossings?
- Has any work been done on this already?
- Will you send me a copy of any relevant reports?
- Which people need to give their permission for a crossing?
- Has any official or councillor been taking an interest in this before?
- What sort of information would be needed to convince you of the necessity of a crossing?
- Who would we present any findings to?

The follow-up letter

Having spoken to the officials concerned, and having received a reply indicating that closure *is* possible or that consideration *is not* being given to providing a crossing, **write a letter.** It is important to include your understanding of the council's position (note the first paragraph of the letter on page 14).

Do it straightaway. Address it to the person in charge of, for example, closing children's playgrounds or the provision of crossings, whose name you will have noted. State simply what you are against (or want) and why. The letter on page 14 is an example of a protest against something being closed, and that on page 15 is an example of an attempt to persuade officials to provide something the community needs.

Of course, as already mentioned, it is not always your local council that you are campaigning against. When we discovered that our child health and well-woman clinic, Amott Road Clinic, was threatened with closure it was our local health authority that we contacted. Our letter to Camberwell Health Authority was like the one on page 16.

Before posting it, you could **take photocopies** of your letter to send to other people who might be interested in your campaign — your ward councillors, for instance, or even your local MP. If you intend to do this put 'cc' followed by their names at the foot of your letter, indicating that you are sending copies to the people named. When sending the copies you could include a covering note asking them for help. But even without a covering letter they will realise that the council, or whoever you have written to, is planning something and that you want something done about it. You can find the addresses of your local MP and councillors at your Citizens' Advice Bureau (CAB) or library.

As with everything you send out from now on, don't forget to **keep a copy** of the letter for your records.

Gathering facts

Having checked your information with the officials concerned, you must now get together some facts to **support your argument.** You will need to show who will be affected by the problem, and how.

Try to visit the site you are campaigning about and actually see what the problems are. Talk to as many people as possible who work in/near/on the site or with the people concerned. Useful, if confidential, information can be gained this way.

If you want to say, for example, that a site is well-used, go and see it at several different times. Try to persuade your MP and councillors, too, and any other eminent person to do likewise — witnesses help.

Ask the officials for the information on which they are basing their action, or non-action. It might take time to get this but if, as we did, you discover that their figures contradict the decision recommended, you will have useful ammunition.

The planning department of your local authority is a good place to find out basic facts about the area, including population, racial mix, proportion of old, young, householders and so on in the area, and information about buildings and roads. The planning office should have the most recent details and statistics available.

If they cannot supply you with the specific facts you need, for example the number of children using the playground each week, go

7, Midfield Road,
Fairfield.
3rd May 1989

Mr J. Bloggs,
Playground Officer,
Parks and Recreation,
Town Hall,
Whytown.

Dear Mr. Bloggs,
    I understand from the telephone conversation that I had with you today that the Council are considering closing the Mill Street Children's playground.
    I wish to register my strong protest at such a move.
    The playground is the nearest play area for my own three children and to many other children in Fairfield. It is well equipped and easy to get to. The equipment is well maintained and safe.
    The nearest other playground is at Ryechester. It is overcrowded with little equipment and involves crossing a dangerous road.
    I urge the Council not to close such a valuable local resource.

Yours sincerely,
Mary Brown (Mrs.)

A follow-up letter registering a protest

34, Midland Road,
Whytown.

9th May 1989

Mrs. Charles
Road Officer
Town Hall,
Whytown.

Dear Mrs. Charles,
    I understand from the telephone conversation that we had today that the Council has no plans at present to provide a pelican crossing outside Whytown Primary School.
    I wish to request in the strongest terms that plans for a crossing be given consideration.
    The school is situated on a busy main road which adults, let alone children, find very hard to cross. There have been a number of serious accidents over the past three months and the lives of any children crossing that road are at risk.
    The crossing patrol person does his best but many motorists take no notice of his sign.
    I would be grateful if you would let me know whether a change of heart on the part of the Council is likely in the near future.

        Yours sincerely,
        John Notts

A follow-up letter attempting persuasion

Mrs J. Aspden   Mrs P. Bird
(Address)   (Address)
                                                 (Date)

SAVE AMOTT ROAD CLINIC CAMPAIGN

Camberwell Services Unit Administrator,
Camberwell Health Authority,
St. Giles Hospital,
St. Giles Road,
London SE5

Dear

We are alarmed to hear about the threatened closure of the Amott Road Clinic. It is used by a lot of people in this area.

There are many women with small children living near the clinic and most of them walk there. The other clinics at Townley Road and Consort Road are too far away to walk to with small children.

It is said that the clinic needs to be closed because it needs repairs. This is not a reason for closing it completely. It should be repaired or moved to the former Thomas Carlton School building in Adys Road which is very close. This building has recently been renovated and has plenty of spare space. An alternative might be the Baptist Church opposite the clinic in Adys Road.

There are a large number of people involved in the Save Amott Road Clinic Campaign. We consider it vital that the clinic remains.

It is to be hoped that everyone will be notified about any form of consultation to take place or which has taken place concerning the clinic and that we will not be presented with a fait accompli.

We hope we can depend upon your support in this matter.

Yours sincerely,

Polly Bird

Polly Bird

out and **get them yourselves.** Stand there each day and do a head count. Find people to cover each part of the day.

Organising a petition is a good way to canvass opinion. You could take the opportunity to ask people a series of questions about the problem so that you can talk with authority about what people think. It is possible to compile a questionnaire for this purpose but this is less effective unless you can be sure that the questions will be unbiased and that a great many people will receive and return it.

When you've gathered as many facts as possible on both sides of the argument, **check them.** Check them with experts (see Chapter 2) and check them against each other. Then you are ready to present an argument to the officials — and the press, if necessary (see page 21).

WHAT TO DO NEXT

So far you have established the nature of the problem by making initial approaches to the decision-making body and by gathering and checking facts. You have made the first moves, but you can't do it all on your own. You have probably found interest among your friends as you have talked to them of your concern. Ask some of them to help you, get together to pool ideas and decide on a plan of action. Those who are interested enough to give of their time will probably form the nucleus of the campaign group.

Your first group meeting

If you have been able to gather together some like-minded people it is important to give each of them something to do straightaway so that they **feel involved** from the beginning and the campaign gets off to a good start. Here are a few things you can be doing as a group at the first meeting:

- clarify your aim
- decide how much time you can spare and how often to meet
- decide on a campaign name
- decide whether you will seek to achieve your aim by private persuasion or public pressure
- ask everyone to write a letter to the officials concerned
- ask everyone to make a list of other people they can approach to write letters, come to the meetings, or make telephone calls
- get everyone to write down a list of other contacts who might be useful, either officials or friends.

Have a clear aim

You may have told officials in your initial approach that you want this or don't want that, but are you clear on your *exact* aim?

What do you want the campaign to do? Keep it **clear and simple:** for example, 'to stop the council closing Mill Street Children's Playground' or 'to get a pelican crossing outside Whytown Primary School'. Abandon any intention to 'bash the council on the way' or 'include clearing up Whytown Park too'. Keep your objective simple, and don't get sidetracked. In our own case we wanted to keep the clinic on or near its original site.

Use your time effectively

Time is a major factor in any campaign. On the one hand there will be a deadline for protestors to meet, and on the other every task connected with running a campaign is time consuming.

You may have a month to protest, or several years. What started out as a short campaign may, because of red tape, drag on for years. Procrastination is a common trick on the part of those in authority. They hope you will get tired of it all and give up. But don't do that — persistence wins.

First decide how much time you can each spare. If one person has a lot of time, but the others can only spare a little each week, then it is probably sensible to ask the first person to be one of the coordinators of the campaign.

How often will you all get together? Perhaps, as for the Save Amott Road Clinic Campaign, once a fortnight will be about right. If things hot up, maybe once a week. If the campaign is likely to go on for years, perhaps once a month. Decide now so that the group has a regular meeting organised.

You can use the telephone to keep in touch with each other, but usually there are papers to be seen or written and this can best be done at a meeting. A meeting also provides an opportunity to pool ideas from many people and to organise who does what next.

Don't start a campaign after the first protest unless you are prepared to give time to it. Nothing looks worse than a campaign which flounders halfway because no-one's got the time to give to it.

Use your time wisely. Read papers at home so that you are ready to discuss them at the meeting. Make lists of points to mention. If and when you become an 'official' campaign you will need an agenda. But even at this stage make sure everyone knows what should be got through at any meeting.

Make every minute count. The officials are paid to put the time in and can afford to wait. You can't afford to waste a minute. If you are asked by the meeting to do something by a certain time, do it. Otherwise you might hold things up.

Choose a name

Officials react to groups differently from the way they do to individuals. When Jeannette telephoned a health authority official at the beginning of our protest, she was asked, 'Who do you represent?' You might think that an individual has as much right to know what is going on as a group does. Officials don't always think so. It made us angry, too.

To be effective, beat them at their own game. We became the 'Save Amott Road Clinic Campaign' (there were only two of us then!) and the official attitude to us changed at once. We became an **interested group** and thus people to be treated with respect and given information and cooperation.

It really doesn't matter what you call the group so long as the name makes clear what you want. If you want to think up clever initials do, but don't waste time on it. You need a name quickly and a simple one is better than none at all.

Announce yourself by your campaign name whenever you speak to officials on the phone. You are then no longer Sheila Smith, just another mum, but Sheila Smith of the 'Save Mill Street Playground Campaign'.

Type the name at the top of your letters. Printed headed paper certainly looks more businesslike if you can afford it, or get someone to provide it (see Chapter 7), but typing the name in capital letters across the top of your letters above the address(es) does just as well. It shows you mean business and officials respond to this.

Appearances are important — always type your letters if possible.

Private persuasion or public pressure

Now you must decide how to achieve your aim. Basically there are two ways, by private persuasion or public pressure. Often you will need a combination of the two.

Private persuasion means writing letters, talking to officials, asking your councillors or MP to intervene. Public pressure means using the press, public meetings, demonstrations and gimmicks to embarrass the opposition by showing the strength of public feeling.

Try **private persuasion** first. There's always a chance that putting forward reasoned argument, with the implied threat of public pressure in the background, may make officials change their minds and find a less objectionable target. Or they might decide, for instance, that money put into a crossing now can be compensated for by a cut in budget in a less controversial area.

Don't feel guilty if you get your way and you hear that someone else is losing out. Fight to win your corner and let other people fight theirs.

On the other hand you may find, as we did, that **public pressure** can speed things up and, by putting them in the public eye, make officials change gear.

However you decide to do it, be clear what methods you are going to use and when. *Make sure everyone else knows.* If you decide to use private persuasion for a few weeks to see how things go, but one of your group informs the press straightaway, you are going to have problems.

Battle for local baby care

PARENTS are campaigning to keep their local baby clinic open. They have been told that the building it occupies is structurally unsound and it may have to close.

Mums say the clinic they take their children to at Amott Road, Peckham, is only five minutes walk from their homes.

Jeanette Aspden, of Oglander Road, Peckham, who has two children, said: "The other clinics are at Townley Road, East Dulwich, and Consort Road, Peckham. It would take us at least 25 minutes with toddlers in tow."

She and her friend Polly Bird have been collecting names for a petition to send to the Camberwell Health Authority and their MP.

Abuse

Mrs Bird has three children, and has used the Amott Road clinic for eight years.

She said: "Child abuse in the area is below average so there must be value in having the clinic here. This is not a political issue. It is vital to the health of the women and children in the area."

The mothers claim the building could be put in good shape if money was spent on it. Failing that there are two other nearby buildings which might be used.

Camberwell Health Authority said: "It would cost around £35,000 to underpin and do basic repairs to the present building. We have not yet reached a decision on what to do."

Deptford & Peckham Mercury, 8 May 1986

Contacting the press

Put out a **press release** as soon as you decide public pressure *is* necessary. The first one should say why you are campaigning, for example, 'Worried mothers in Fairfield have protested to the council about the proposal to close Mill Street Playground'. As you gather more facts they can go in later press releases. The result of one of our early press releases is shown on the previous page.

GETTING ORGANISED

Organisation is what keeps a campaign **running smoothly.** It is the way you keep track of what is happening and how you make sure everyone is working effectively. However, if you are not careful, organisation can become an end in itself. You can become more concerned with the finer points of meetings and papers than in running the campaign effectively. Or you can spend so long forming a properly-constituted group that you don't do anything until it's too late.

But each campaign needs to be well organised. It needs to be run as **efficiently** as possible so that everyone knows what they are supposed to be doing. If the *mechanics* of campaigning are taken care of, then everyone can concentrate on the *aim*.

You will need to think about:

● size
● officers needed
● constitution
● standing orders
● running a meeting
● where to hold meetings
● subscriptions
● what to do with records
● legal and insurance aspects.

SIZE

Right at the start decide on how many people you need to cope with the day-to-day **running of the campaign.** The campaign group is best kept as small as possible — the fewer people in charge of the day-to-day running of the campaign the better. If every decision needs to be agreed by twenty people it will obviously take longer and you may miss an important deadline. The more people trying to run something, the greater chances there are of internal bickering, rather than decision-making.

The meetings themselves could be limited to ten or twelve people so that you can meet in a private house. A **regular newsletter** could be the means of communicating decisions made to the rest of those interested.

Decide how decisions are going to be taken. Are you in favour of **collective decision-making** and, if so, will you act on a vote or reach a consensus? Or will one person act as **leader** and make all decisions unless challenged by the rest of the group? The best arrangement is to have two or three coordinators who can be empowered to take decisions between the meetings if necessary. This can be done by telephone, which is rather more difficult if more than three people are involved. The Save Amott Road Clinic Campaign had two joint coordinators.

Sheila and Mary decide to be joint chairwomen of the Save Mill Street Playground Campaign, while John wants to be unchallenged leader of the Build Whytown School Crossing Movement.

OFFICERS

Although some jobs can be combined, even a small group will need a few officers just to make sure things run smoothly. If you get to the point of applying to the local council or other body for a **grant,** then they will probably have rules about the number of officers you will need and how the group is to be run.

Some groups like to rotate the various jobs at every meeting but this can cause problems if the next person on the rota does not turn up. Another difficulty is that no-one gets a chance to learn the job. It can take time to become a firm chairman or efficient secretary. It is also confusing to the public and officials you are dealing with if you have different officers at each meeting. Try to keep officers in their jobs for a reasonable length of time.

If you have a group bank account you will need a minimum of two signatures in order to stop one person running off to Bermuda with the money. The **signatories** must be officers of the group, usually the chairman and treasurer.

Chairman
Sometimes called the chair or chairperson, this is the person who **runs the meetings** and keeps them in order. He or she is the person people look to to guide them and to comment on the group's activities so needs to be an active organiser.

Some people holding strong views about discrimination might find the term 'chairman' offensive (the terms 'chair' or 'chairperson' do not have a wide appeal either). If this is the case in your group, why not use an alternative term such as 'coordinator'? The term chairman is used here in order to be consistent.

Vice-chairman

You don't really need a vice-chairman in a small group because anyone can **deputise for the chairman** if the group agrees. But it saves delays and argument if there is one person to turn to when the chairman is unavailable. The role of vice-chairman can be combined with another.

Treasurer

This is the person who **looks after the money** and keeps detailed records of receipts and payments. The job is not as difficult as it sounds; you don't need to find someone with an accountancy or book-keeping background, just a person of integrity and honesty. The job can be combined with another but is best kept separate. More information on recording money transactions is given in Chapter 6.

Secretary

The secretary has the hard work and the person doing this job should be willing and able to spare a lot of **time and effort.** This is a job which could be given to a different person each year because it can be exhausting.

The secretary has to make notes of what was discussed and decided at any meeting, write any official letters from the group, send out newsletters if necessary, and let everyone know when the next meeting will be. He or she also has to deal with any correspondence to the campaign. It is a key job, as is that of the chairman, and it is not advisable to combine this job with any other because of the work involved.

Other officers

There may be other jobs that the campaign group feels would be useful, such as:

● newsletter editor
● newsletter distribution organiser
● membership secretary
● publicity officer
● events organiser

Write down a list of all the jobs you think need to be done. Then write down a list of people whom you could ask to do the jobs, and match them up. They might not want to do them, of course, but it's worth trying. If you know people who would like to do particular jobs, it is much better to ask them rather than to press unwilling people to do them.

Typical responsibilities of the officers

Chairman (and/or vice-chairman)

Open group meetings
Introduce and welcome visitors and speakers
Read out minutes of previous meeting and sign an accurate
    record
Make sure the agenda is followed
Control hecklers
Sum up meetings
Liaise with other local groups
Act as group spokesman for press contacts (if not covered
    by a **Publicity officer)**
Give talks (if not done by a **Publicity officer)**

Secretary

Keep notes of meetings
Draw up and circulate agendas (in consultation with the
    Chairman)
Type up and circulate minutes
Write and post official letters
Keep proper files of all correspondence and copies of all
    documents
Organise mailshots — printing, address labels etc (if not
    done by a **Publicity officer)**

Treasurer

Keep any books of account
Bank cash and maintain bank account
Keep chequebook and other bank books
Make payments as required
Draw up annual accounts
Liaise with auditors
Collect membership fees and renewals (if not done by a
    Membership secretary)

Newsletter editor

Plan the contents of the newsletter
Find good contributors and commission their contributions
Write pieces to fill gaps
Obtain any drawings or photographs for illustrations
Prepare the layout of the newsletter
Get competitive quotes from local printers
Check proofs and send the edition to press
Circulate finished copies (if not done by a **Newsletter distribution organiser)**

Membership secretary

Encourage people to join
Keep a file or register of members
Issue membership cards
Collect membership fees and renewals

Publicity officer/Events organiser

Draw up publicity plans for the committee
Organise media coverage (press, radio, TV)
Other public relations
Attend meetings, make visits, give talks
Get t-shirts, badges, stickers, etc, made
Organise promotional demonstrations and events
Organise mailshots

CONSTITUTION

A constitution is a statement setting out rules for governing the group, and includes details of its aims and objectives, its membership, the standing orders and AGM (Annual General Meeting).

Do you need a constitution? For the purposes of getting started, no. A simple **statement of your aims** is adequate. Something like 'The aim of the Save Mill Street Playground Campaign is to stop the closure of Mill Street Children's Playground' would suffice. Make sure all your supporters know what the aim is and what it means.

To run informal meetings you just need someone to make a list of things to be discussed and to choose someone to chair the meeting. But if you have been given a grant or other form of official help, then you will need a proper constitution, drawn up in such a way as to satisfy not only the grant-giving body but also its lawyers.

If you are applying for a grant and are not sure what is needed in a constitution, **ask advice** from the body which is considering giving you the grant. They will be pleased to tell you what each section involves and help you with the wording. They will know what their lawyers require, so don't be afraid to ask. We asked about wording and rules and received a lot of support from the people involved. They even advised us to change our name slightly.

Most constitutions are similar in form and content. Our constitution is shown on the next page so that you can see what we did. It was carefully worded to allow for the fact that there were only two official coordinators but a lot of volunteers, very few of whom were willing to turn up to regular meetings.

Keep your constitution as **flexible** as the lawyers will allow in case your support fluctuates. It is no good having rules about a minimum voting group (quorum) of ten if you only get three people to to an important meeting.

STANDING ORDERS

The rules laid down in the constitution about how the group should be run, that is who can be on the management committee, when and how to elect officers, how often to meet, the number making a quorum, who will make decisions and how, are known as **standing orders**. These should be decided before regular formal meetings take place. You will need these anyway if you are receiving any grant.

You will find that any group of a reasonable size, perhaps more than twelve, will find it easier to operate with more formal rules. Keep these rules to a minimum and be careful to make them as flexible as allowed. If possible, appoint all members to the management committee, as in

SAVE AMOTT ROAD CLINIC PROJECT
CONSTITUTION

NAME
The group will be known as the 'Save Amott Road Clinic Project'.

AIMS & OBJECTIVES
The aim of the Save Amott Road Clinic Project is to save the Amott Road Clinic with the help of such activities as letters, petitions, leaflets, press releases, talks, presentation of papers and perhaps conferences and exhibitions.

MEMBERSHIP
Membership consists of two coordinators who operate with the help of local volunteers.

STANDING ORDERS
1. Members of the Save Amott Road Clinic Project shall constitute the management committee of the organisation.
2. The Group shall elect a Secretary and a Treasurer each year at the Annual General Meeting.
3. The Group will hold a general meeting at least once a month. Members will be notified of the time and place of meetings, and the agenda, at least five days before the meeting.
4. No decision can be taken at any general meeting of the group unless two members are present.
5. Between meetings, the Treasurer and Secretary can make decisions which cannot be deferred until a general meeting is called. Any such decision will be ratified at the next general meeting.

ANNUAL GENERAL MEETING
An Annual General Meeting shall be held each year within three months of the end of the financial year. This meeting will:

(a) review the work of the group;
(b) approve audited accounts;
(c) elect a Treasurer and Secretary;
(d) nominate auditors for the following year.

A sample constitution

the example shown, so that meetings can go ahead with whoever is there.

The following items should be in any constitution and standing orders.

Membership

Make the membership as open as possible within the conditions imposed by any grant-giving body. **Don't exclude any section of the community** on the grounds of race, sex, religion, age, or disability. If you are asked on the form whether you are including certain sections of the community on your management committee be honest. We had to say that although we didn't exclude people with disabilities we didn't provide special access to the committee rooms because these were just ordinary homes. We still got our grant.

How many members do you need? As many as you can get! But don't be surprised if many people express an interest, fewer become members and even fewer turn up to meetings. Keep everyone informed about what is going on and don't hesitate to ask everyone for help.

Election of officers

You will need to **elect the officers** for the group before meetings can be conducted. Elect the chairman first so that he or she can take charge of the rest of the elections and the meeting. Then elect the vice-chairman, if you are going to have one, and then the treasurer and secretary. Finally, elect any other officers. The yearly meeting at which the officers are elected is called the AGM (Annual General Meeting).

Frequency of meetings

How often you should meet will depend a lot on the enthusiasm of the group and the needs of the campaign. Once a week or fortnight might be all right when things are very busy. Once a month is adequate for official purposes and if the campaign is likely to go on for years. Only make it more frequent than that if really necessary because people will resent a large call on their time when there is nothing specific for them to do.

Quorum

You will need to decide what **minimum number** of members is needed before a meeting can start (a quorum). Make the quorum for a meeting as low as you are allowed to, otherwise you might not be able to conduct any business if you get small numbers for several meetings when, for example, the weather is very cold.

Who takes decisions?

Decide who can take decisions between meetings. Two or three people will be enough, preferably with telephones so that they can contact each other easily. Perhaps the secretary, treasurer and chairman, or the chairman and two ordinary members. You need to include one of the **officers** so that they can act as a representative of the campaign.

AGM

The AGM is the Annual General Meeting of a group at which **new officers** are elected for the following year. Usually the AGM is at the end of the financial year. Short **reports** might be needed from each existing officer for submission to interested parties, such as your sponsor, or the grant-giving body. If you have audited accounts these will need to be approved by the members at the AGM. Even if there is no requirement that they be audited, the **accounts** should be made available for inspection by any member. They should be up to date. If necessary at the AGM the group will need to nominate **auditors** for the next year. See Chapter 6 for more about finances.

RUNNING A MEETING

Now that you have decided on the preliminary organisation, you will need to know how to organise your meetings. You will need to think about an agenda, minutes, motions and discussion.

Agenda

Even if you are running things on an informal basis, you will still need to have an order of business for the meeting. The agenda should make provision for discussing and approving the minutes, or notes, of the last meeting, giving details of correspondence, and should list any other matters to be discussed by the group.

Before each meeting the secretary, in consultation with the chairman, will need to produce the agenda. Make **copies** for everyone and make sure they get distributed at least one week before each meeting. If you have more frequent meetings or lots of members this may well prove impracticable. In that case at least have copies of the agenda for everyone who comes to the meeting.

Minutes

Someone must **take notes** of what was discussed and decided at all the meetings. This is usually the secretary's job, if the campaign has one, but anyone can do it. The resulting notes are called minutes and are the only record of what the meeting was about.

SAVE MILL STREET PLAYGROUND CAMPAIGN

AGENDA
of meeting to be held at 19 Barton Close,
Fairfield on Tuesday 4th April 1989 at 6.00 p.m.

1 Apologies for absence

2 Minutes of meeting of 2nd March 1989

3 Matters arising from the minutes

4 Correspondence

5 Treasurer's report

6 Business: (a) Leafletting Down Street School
            (b) Jumble sale

7 Any other business

8 Date and time of next meeting

A typical agenda

You don't have to record every word in an argument, just record that, for example, 'a heated discussion took place' and what the decision was. Keep the notes short but accurate because they must be approved by members at the following meeting as a true record of that meeting. Copies of the minutes should go to every member, but this could be reduced to copies for members who come to the meetings.

If at the next meeting someone wants to **change the minutes** because they are inaccurate, the correction must be written in straightaway. When the minutes are decided upon as being a correct record of the previous meeting, the chairman must sign a copy of them straightaway, and the copies are kept in case anyone wants to check what happened at a particular meeting.

Motions
A motion is a **formal proposal** put to the group, laying down a change in the rules, or a course of action to be taken, or something to which the agreement of the whole group is required. If someone puts forward a motion at least one person must support it, or **second** it. Record it word for word in the notes or minutes. Then when a vote is taken on it, record the result.

SAVE MILL STREET PLAYGROUND CAMPAIGN

MINUTES
of the meeting held on Tuesday 4th April 1989, at
19 Barton Close, Fairfield at 6.00 p.m.

Present: Mary Brown (Joint Chairwoman), Jemima Green, John Harris (Secretary), Mary Newtown, Hilda Open (Treasurer), Amanda Legs, Sheila Smith (Joint Chairwoman), Frank Tees.

Apologies for absence: Pamela Agis, Hilary Derton.

Minutes of the meeting held on Tuesday 2nd March 1989, were read and confirmed.

Matters arising: There were no matters arising.

Correspondence:
To: (a)   Cllr Thomas requesting that he address the campaign on a date convenient to him.

From: (a)   Cllr Alders re a meeting with M. Brown and F. Tees.   (Secretary to confirm date)
        (b)   Leaflet re Pre-School Playgroup coffee morning on 4th May.   (For information)

Treasurer's report: The campaign's balance stands in credit at £51.34. There are no outstanding bills.

New business:
(1) Leafletting Down Street School. M. Brown reported that she had received the leaflets from the printers. J. Harris agreed to help with the distribution outside the school on Friday morning, 7th April.

(2) Jumble sale. There was a heated discussion about the necessity for a sale. Motion: THAT INSTEAD OF A JUMBLE SALE A COFFEE MORNING BE HELD ON SATURDAY 29th JULY, 1989. Mover — S. Smith. Seconder — H. Open. Carried.

Any other business: M. Brown reminded everyone about the One-O'Clock Club open afternoon on 29th April.

Date and time of next meeting: Tuesday 2nd May at 6.00 p.m.

There being no further business the meeting closed at 8.45 p.m.

Confirmed: Mary Brown (Chairwoman)
        Sheila Smith (Chairwoman)

        4th April, 1989

Typical minutes of meeting

Some typical motions

'That the annual subscription fee be raised by £5 to £15 for members over 21.'

'That Ms Smith be appointed organiser for the demonstration to be held in March.'

'That a complaint should be lodged with the printers of the newsletter for the poor quality of printing, and a refund of £75 requested.'

'That no persons under 18 shall be admitted as members.'

'That a vote of thanks be passed for the Secretary in recognition of his hard work during the previous year.'

Discussion

The chairman must try to let everyone have their say without unduly holding up the meeting. It is not wise to let the meeting go on too long, because people get tired and bored and cannot concentrate properly. If there is too much to be discussed in a reasonable time, about two hours, then another meeting could be called, or a **sub-committee** of some of the members could be formed to talk about the additional matters on another occasion.

WHERE TO HOLD MEETINGS

A room in someone's house is the ideal place to hold a meeting — perhaps organised on a rota system — but if you get a large number of people at each meeting you might have to consider hiring or borrowing a hall or room. Try asking the local church, school, youth club or public house. Avoid such an arrangement if at all possible because it is depressing and offputting to sit in a cold, strange, often bare room or hall. Even if chairs can be arranged in a group or circle, the atmosphere is rarely relaxing. If you suddenly get a drop in membership the cost of the room is wasted.

Try to make meetings **comfortable.** Contrary to popular belief, people are unlikely to go to sleep if given a comfortable chair and a warm, pleasant room in which to discuss things. They are more likely to give up coming to meetings if the chairs are hard and the room is cold and bleak.

Tips for good venues

If your meetings grow in size, or you hold larger meetings open to the public, and you do have to consider hiring a room or hall, try to make sure that as many as possible of the following **facilities** are available:

- Car parking
- Accessible for public transport
- Warm room
- Away from traffic or other distracting noise
- Comfortable seating
- Good acoustics
- Good light to see by
- Provision if possible for disabled to attend
- Toilet facilities
- Space to display material
- Varied simple refreshments
- Pay telephone facility.

Checklist of possible meeting places	
Venue	*Address*
Private house	_____
	_____
Church hall	_____
	_____
Community Centre	_____
	_____
School hall	_____
	_____
Town Hall	_____
	_____
Sports Centre	_____
	_____
Political club	_____
	_____
Social club	_____
	_____
Other	_____
	_____

SUBSCRIPTIONS

These are regular payments by members to campaign funds, sometimes paid monthly, but more usually once a year.

If you can do without them, do, because they might put people off. If you do need extra money and want to raise it from subscriptions, keep the sum as small as possible in order not to deter people. Ideally, try to get your money by other means, such as **donations,** especially if the campaign is likely to be a short one.

Donations often bring in more money. Try the occasional plea for cash to fund a special project, for example, money for a special leaflet, and you will probably do quite well.

KEEPING YOUR RECORDS

It is vital to **keep copies of everything** so that you can check on any piece of information. It is no good, for example, sending out information to your opponents and then being unable to check what you said to them when asked for a quote by the press. The secretary should keep documents related to the group. Make sure that anyone sending out campaign documents gives copies to the secretary so all the information is in one place.

You will need to keep copies of:

- accounts
- minutes
- each agenda
- each letter from the campaign to members
- each letter from the campaign to anyone else
- each letter sent to the campaign group
- press cuttings concerning the campaign
- press cuttings about relevant subjects
- notes of telephone calls concerning the campaign
- lists of useful addresses and telephone numbers
- lists of members' addresses and phone numbers
- lists of official addresses and phone numbers
- addresses and phone numbers of the press
- each press release the campaign puts out
- each poster the campaign uses
- each campaign leaflet
- tapes of any TV or radio programme where your campaign has been mentioned (if you're lucky!).

All this may sound as if you need a huge filing system and loads of time. You don't. Buy two **box files** and a few **plastic folders.** Put all the correspondence in plastic folders in one box, separated into letters received and those sent. Put everything else in the other box. Addresses should be kept in a simple address book. That's all. Never make a filing system more important than the campaign.

Stick **press cuttings** onto sheets of paper, write the date and the name of the paper it came from on the sheet. Keep the sheets in a loose leaf folder. This makes it easy to photocopy the cuttings.

All documents to do with the finances of the campaign must be kept by the treasurer. Again a box file is all that is necessary to hold the account books, receipts and so on.

CAMPAIGNING AND THE LAW

Don't let anyone persuade the campaign to break the law. Besides possible costs in terms of fines or imprisonment, it would bring adverse publicity, reduce cooperation from the police and other official bodies, and be off-putting for the majority of your supporters who will be law-abiding citizens.

It is sensible to find out during the early stages of a campaign what the legal implications are. You may have a legal expert amongst your supporters. If not, try to find someone locally who can give you impartial advice on legal and insurance matters (see Chapter 2). Some of the basic issues are outlined below.

Will the law affect our constitution?

Your campaign might simply have a set of basic rules, but once it needs to raise money, employ staff (perhaps a part-time secretary), or own property, then it takes on legal and managerial responsibilities and your constitution should define who meets these obligations.

You are not legally bound to register your constitution, but if you don't you are an **unregistered association.** As such your campaign group has no legal identity of its own and individuals have to be nominated to act on behalf of the campaign to hold property or to deal with the finances. Although such a campaign is less constrained by the law and can more easily be wound up, it does mean that individuals on the management committee are held *personally responsible* for the campaign's obligations and debts, and as such could find themselves being sued for something which was not directly their fault.

To avoid this the campaign could become a **limited company.** It would then have its own legal identity and could, among other things, sue and be sued and own property. However, it would have to obey rules set out by the various Companies Acts and submit details of its affairs and accounts to the Registrar of Companies. Its constitution would have to be in a particular form to satisfy the Companies Acts.

A limited company can be started by a minimum of two people. Each member is asked to contribute a small sum (which can be as little as £5 each) and this is normally the limit of their liability if anything goes wrong.

For information on how to register under the **Companies Act 1985,** write to the Registrar of Companies, Companies Registration Office (CRO), Crown House, Crown Way, Maindy, Cardiff CF4 3UZ (tel: 0222-388588), 102 George Street, Edinburgh EH2 3DJ (for Scotland), or IDB House, 64 Chichester Street, Belfast BT1 4JX (for Northern Ireland).

Do we need insurance?

If you meet in members' homes then they must make sure that they each have **household insurance** which covers accidents and loss of property, including money, to or belonging to people on their premises.

When you hold meetings in another place, such as a hall, check that the owner has an **insurance policy** which would cover such a possibility as the hall burning down through the negligence of one of your members. If not, ask the owner to extend his policy at your expense to cover you as users of the building.

You should take out **public liability insurance** to cover injury, loss or damage as a result of any negligence on the part of the organisers, and this can be extended quite cheaply to cover all types of public liability. You might want to consider getting **all risks and accidental damage insurance** if the campaign has property, such as a photocopier, which might be moved between premises or lent to other people.

If your campaign is an unincorporated group, an individual must be nominated to take out any insurance on its behalf.

Insurance can be bought directly from an insurance company or through a broker. The British Insurance Brokers Association can provide details of registered brokers for each area. Contact it at BIBA House, 14 Bevis Marks, London EC3 7NT (tel: 01-623 9043). Otherwise ask other local voluntary groups to recommend someone.

Have we got a right to demonstrate?

A campaign has no special *right* to meet and demonstrate. Meetings and demonstrations are only legal if they do not break the law.

No meeting can be held without permission or prior notice. If a meeting is to be held on private property, then the **owner's permission** must be obtained. Otherwise the people at the meeting will technically be trespassers and could be sued for any loss or damage occurring. If the meeting is held on public property there may be a **local bylaw** or **Act** requiring a certain minimum time for notification to the police and local authority.

What do the police need to know?
The **Public Order Act 1986** concerns any assembly of twenty or more people. If such a group wishes to hold a **march or procession** in a public place they must give seven days' notice to the police. If the march is to be organised within that time limit, then as much notice as possible must be given. The police must know the date, starting time, and route of the procession, together with the name and address of one of the organisers. If there are any changes to this information, it is an offence not to inform the police.

The police have powers to impose conditions on where and how the march is conducted so it is sensible to liaise with them as early as possible and to follow their advice. When approached courteously and in good time the police are generally helpful and cooperative. Their local knowledge can be useful, too.

What is a breach of the peace?
Anything which disturbs the 'preservation of law and order' is an offence. Usually there must be some force or threat of force involved before someone is held to have committed an offence. Offences range from minor assaults, threats or obstructions, to riot and affray. A person committing one of the more serious offences will usually be charged with that offence. When no *crime* has been committed the lesser charge of committing a **breach of the peace** is used. If the Build Whytown School Crossing Movement and its opponents shout slogans at each other no specific offence is committed, but if tempers rise and people become abusive or threatening this could be a breach of the peace.

Anyone found guilty of a breach of the peace will be bound over to keep the peace or to be of good behaviour. If he refuses to comply he can be sent to prison.

When would we be obstructing the highway?
The highway, including the pavement, is for 'passing and repassing'. Holding a meeting or march would be an offence if it stopped this. Even stopping to talk to a friend on the pavement is technically breaking the law. However, the police do not usually prosecute if, as in this case, the action is reasonable.

The charge is vague and the police can use it for immediate arrest without a warrant, so it is commonly used against demonstrators. It might be safer to have a **moving procession** rather than a meeting so that participants can argue that they are 'passing and repassing'. This is why demonstrators wishing to block a road sometimes do so by walking backwards and forwards across a zebra crossing. However, the police may still decide to test how reasonable this is in court.

When could we be charged with unlawful assembly?

If three or more people meet **intending** to do something that might cause a breach of the peace, ie lead to violence, then it is an offence. It is a charge which can be brought against people holding a counter-demonstration when the police expect trouble.

Can we put up our posters anywhere?

No. Sticking up posters in public places is illegal under the **Town and Country Planning Acts** and often under local bylaws too. If Mary wants to go out at night and stick up posters on lampposts about the Save Mill Street Playground Campaign coffee morning she is breaking the law — **flyposting** — and, if caught, could be fined in a magistrates' court.

She would be within the law if she wished to advertise a non-commercial event, such as a campaign meeting, and had the **permission** of the owner of the place where she wished to put the poster, such as a hoarding. But even in those circumstances there are usually other detailed requirements, such as the size of the poster, which she would need to find out about from her local authority.

What are slander and libel?

Under English law slander is **spoken** defamation of character, and libel is a malicious publication or **written** defamation. So if you say or write anything that could damage someone's reputation and the facts are wrong you could be sued. This could still be the case if you are quoting someone else. Even if you don't name the person, if they can be identified by the context it is still possible for you to be sued.

The best thing to do is not to say or print anything that could be considered slander or libel. Check any leaflets or press releases before they go out for anything that could be libellous and don't indulge in personal accusations when speaking on behalf of the campaign. If you have an experienced journalist or solicitor amongst your members who can advise you, so much the better.

Will our fund-raising break the law?

There are no formal requirements for raising funds from your members or for holding small fund-raising events. But you must get approval from your **local authority** if you want to do house-to-house collections, street collections, or large-scale gambling and raffles.

Chapter checklist

- Don't wait — start now.
- Find out who makes the decisions about the problem.
- Establish the true facts about the problem.
- Write a letter
  - summarise your understanding of the official position
  - say how you want it changed
  - send copies to other interested people.
- Find others to help you.
- Organise your first meeting.
- Clarify your aim.
- Establish timescales.
- Choose a name.
- Decide how you will achieve your aim.
- Decide how many people are needed to cope with the day-to-day running of the campaign.
- Elect officers.
- Decide how decisions will be made.
- Draw up a simple constitution — get help with the wording if necessary.
- Make sure standing orders are flexible and aid the smooth running of the campaign.
- Make sure meetings are properly organised and well run.
- Decide where to hold meetings and locate alternative venues in case circumstances change.
- Decide whether you will raise money by subscriptions or rely upon donations and fund-raising activities.
- Make sure full records are kept, and kept safely.
- Get professional advice about insurance requirements.
- Ensure that all campaign activities stay within the law — take legal advice if necessary.
- Always cooperate with the police so that they will cooperate with you.

2
Getting Help

WHO CAN HELP?

Without help from other people you have no campaign. One letter or telephone call of protest from you might get a campaign started, but it needs other people to keep it going. The fact that other people are willing to support you adds weight to your arguments. People are your most valuable resource.

Who can you ask to help? Simply, anyone who you think can help you. Be ruthless — bully people into helping, appeal to their conscience, their sense of justice. Convince them you're right. **Be persistent** until you get what you want, whether a letter of support or someone to wear a badge.

The trick is to know what to ask of whom. Who can you ask? People to try include:

- friends
- supporters
- MPs
- councillors
- officials
- experts.

FRIENDS

You may not get as much help from your friends as you had hoped. What seemed at first to them to be an admirable cause and an interesting topic of conversation while someone else was dealing with it (that is, you) might later seem tiresome if they are suddenly asked to help. So don't expect more than a few to want the responsibility of organisation, meetings, decisions, and so on. Those who are willing, use ruthlessly.

Other friends might give other less committed forms of help such as:

- writing a letter of protest or support
- wearing a badge
- displaying a poster
- turning up at social/fund raising events
- signing a petition.

If you want letters written, don't be afraid to suggest what could be written.

Friends are sometimes experts, of course. Are any of them professional or amateur:

- **accountants,** perhaps willing to do the yearly audit?
- **lawyers,** for free advice?
- **artists,** who could design, if not print, badges, posters, t-shirts?
- **printers,** for cheap printing?
- **architects,** for free or cheap advice if a building is at the centre of the campaign?
- **officials** in any organisation, who could steer you through red tape?

Most people have some sort of talent, even if they are only experts at filling envelopes!

Don't be afraid to ask for help from your friends in their official capacity. In many ways it is easier for them to use their official expertise occasionally for the campaign, rather than have to be committed long term organisers or supporters.

Don't ever forget that where even the smallest amount of help or support is given by friends they must receive **praise and thanks** (as must everyone else who helps you). The fact that they are friends is no excuse to ignore the basic courtesies. If praised, friends may be willing to give more help later.

Before you go on, make a list of friends who might be willing to help and make a note of any **special skills** they have that the campaign could use.

SUPPORTERS

Supporters are people, not necessarily well known to you, who in general terms agree with the aims of your campaign and wish it to do well.

How can you contact them? One way is to put a leaflet through every door in the area, another is to write to all potential supporters or organisations which might represent them. A lot depends on whether your potential supporters are a whole community or a particular section of that community.

In the case of the Amott Road Clinic, our immediate supporters were the parents, mostly mothers of under-fives who used the child health clinic, and women who used or were likely to use the well-woman clinic. In fact, the importance of the health and wellbeing of women and children is so fundamental to the community as a whole that we had support from all over the area, from all kinds of people.

Mary and Sheila's supporters for saving the playground are the local parents. John's supporters for getting a crossing are the parents and teachers of the local school and local residents, especially elderly people.

Originally Jeannette and I wrote to all the organisations and groups concerned with women and pre-school children in the area. We also contacted churches of all denominations, and any local school — approaching both headteachers and chairmen of PTAs (Parent Teacher Associations) — whose children might have attended the clinic.

The response was not as good as we had hoped. This was because we had been too ambitious. We asked people to write and protest and send a copy of their letter to us, sign a petition to be forwarded to us, and to display a poster.

This serves as a warning to **keep it simple.** Ask people to display a poster. That's easy. Then ask if you can speak to their group. This takes the obligation away from them and means that you are on hand to encourage people to fill in a petition form after your talk. People are more likely to fill in a petition when there is someone there to put the pen in their hands. This arrangement works particularly well with political groups who like to have speakers.

Once you have located your supporters, keep them informed by means of letters or press releases. People like to feel involved, even if they are not active in a campaign. If you do not keep people's interest they will stop supporting you.

MEMBERS OF PARLIAMENT

As soon as your campaign is taking shape and has a clear aim and a name, the coordinators should write to the local Member of Parliament (MP) asking for support. It is easier for your MP to work out who you are and what you want if he has your letter in front of him. Then follow this up by arranging a meeting when the MP holds his or her **advice surgery,** that is, the regular local session when the MP meets members of the public and listens to their problems. Find out where and when this is being held from your local Citizens' Advice Bureau (CAB) or library.

If you have presented your case well, your MP will probably support you. If he or she does not, don't despair. Ask a sympathetic MP in a neighbouring constituency. Our MP was active in supporting our campaign, but, as you can see from page 44, we also had support from two neighbouring MPs from different political parties. This can be a great help with publicity.

What can you ask your MP to do?

- Write a letter of protest.
- Ask officials for information and perhaps documents that they might not otherwise show you.
- Get other people to put pressure on from above.
- Advise you about appropriate wording and presentation of a petition and then present it to Parliament.
- Ask questions in Parliament.
- Give you advice about what you could do next.
- Suggest contacts.
- Lend his or her name to any publicity.

In return, **acknowledge your MP's help** in any press releases; he or she will certainly use involvement in your campaign in their own publicity. Keep your MP up to date with your activities so that they don't come as a surprise to him or her.

Don't worry if your politics are not those of your MP. Your MP is there to help any constituent, whatever their political party. You are not going to make a political issue out of it, so don't discuss the politics, just the case in hand. Jeannette has no vote and I have different views from my MP but he nevertheless gave us his help. We didn't harangue him about his politics, merely told him about the campaign.

Prospective MPs

Don't forget prospective MPs, too. One of them may be your next MP and they will want to encourage your support. They can also write letters, get the campaign publicity and put pressure on officials, particularly if they are well-known locally. Again, keep them informed and acknowledge help where possible.

COUNCILLORS

These are important people to contact as soon as possible. They can raise the subject of your campaign at their local political **ward meetings** and arrange for motions to be passed supporting your campaign. Copies can then be sent to your opponents and this will increase the pressure on them, especially if the motions are reported to the papers. More information about how councils work is given in Chapter 5.

Councillors can also encourage their political ward to write official-

ALL PARTY SUPPORT FOR CLINIC CAMPAIGN

SOUTHWARK'S Tory, Labour and Liberal MPs have cast aside political differences in a bid to save a clinic which serves 11,000 people in East Dulwich and Peckham.

By James Barcock

Gerald Bowden (Tory, Dulwich), Harriett Harman (Labour, Peckham) and Simon Hughes (Liberal, Bermondsey) are all supporting the Save Amott Road Clinic Campaign, which is being run by two worried mothers.

Camberwell Health Authority want to close the clinic for repairs, but the campaigners believe they really want to shut it down permanently to save money.

The idea is to "temporarily" make patients use the Townley Road clinic, but campaign organiser Jeanette Aspden points out that it would take mothers with children 25 minutes to walk to that clinic.

"It is a totally unsatisfactory move", she said this week.

Southwark Council voted unanimously to support the campaign and have decided to offer the health authority land in Bellenden Ward to site a temporary clinic.

The campaign organisers have also found an empty building a few doors away from the present clinic which could be rented.

Mrs Aspden, a mother of two, admits the clinic needs repairing, but she says: "With these two alternatives there is no need to move the clinic out of the area.

The clinic was originally due to close in June, but the campaigners managed to delay that.

The MPs are continuing to apply pressure to health chiefs.

Mr Bowden has presented a petition to the House of Commons and is lobbying the health authority.

Simon Hughes says: "This campaign needs all the encouragement possible, especially in light of declining hospt.l provisions."

Harriett Harman has told campaign organisers: "I share your concern. I will do everything I can to save your very much needed service."

A Camberwell Health Authority spokeswoman said: "No decision has been made about Amott Road Clinic. The clinic has structural problems that need a lot of money to repair. The clinic though, is quite safe for the next six months and will not close during that time or be pulled down.

"We always listen to the views of the general public."

ly to your opponents supporting the campaign and they can raise the subject at **council meetings**. One of our councillors put forward a motion supporting the campaign to save the Amott Road Clinic at a full council meeting and it got the unanimous support of councillors from all political parties — an almost unheard of event. In any case a motion supporting your campaign would bring the subject to the attention of all councillors. Those not present would see it on their copies of the minutes for that meeting.

● Don't forget to contact prospective councillors in the area if an election is near.
● Keep your councillors informed. They can't help you if they don't know the latest situation about the campaign.
● Praise their help and thank them for it. Mention them by name in press releases when they have given you help. This helps your publicity and gives them kudos.

If you think your councillors are not giving you the help they could, don't be afraid to nag them. They are very busy people, but it is your business to make sure that your campaign is given their time.

OFFICIALS

Do not confuse these with politicians or councillors. **Officials** run the organisations for the benefit of the public and their bosses, for example, council officials carry out decisions made by councillors representing local voters. Some officials will be on your side and some against you. Both sides have their uses.

For example, John is demanding a pelican crossing outside Whytown Primary School. He can see the traffic is dangerous and has done traffic counts but the council say it's not dangerous enough to justify a crossing. Without supporting evidence the council won't spend the money on a crossing there. He asks the council for their own figures. They haven't done a traffic survey themselves, so he puts pressure on them to do so to justify their opposition. When their survey is done he obtains a copy in order to see if any of it can be reinterpreted as support for the crossing. For example, if the survey says 'X cars per hour use the road' John can quote them and say, 'Council figures show that X cars per hour use the road. This is surely a dangerous number, especially as most of them are travelling at speed where children need to cross the road'. So officials who seemed to be opposing his campaign have in fact provided ammunition for it!

Similarly, we asked the health authority for their own figures for attendances at our clinics and the planning department of the council

for information about the local population. We found that the health
authority's own figures proved our case for a clinic rather than their
own for moving it. In fact it was doing the work of two equivalent
clinics in a neighbouring ward — we actually needed more clinics rather
than no clinic.

Official information

This is usually not difficult to come by. Most of it is available to the
public eventually, if the public asks for it. It is surprising how many
official documents you may see, although the publicity about them is
minimal.

If, of course, you receive information **unofficially** that is not available
to the public, never reveal your source (your 'mole') and never admit
to having seen it.

Be careful how you use unauthorised information. If you discover
that an organisation is planning to demolish a building and sell the land
for a certain sum of money, you could ask a question of officials like
this:

- 'Supposing one idea was to demolish the building and sell the land.
  That might raise several thousand pounds. But we would prefer
  another idea, that is . . .'

This would make it clear that you know what is intended without actually admitting it.

Always check your opponent's facts and figures if you can get hold
of them. Use them if possible. Very rarely are factual reports denied
you although internal reports might be.

Making contact with officials

Other officials you could contact are

- secretaries of council committees
- officers in charge of council departments
- the Public Relations Officer (PRO) of an organisation
- the development section of an organisation
- police
- headteachers
- doctors
- lawyers

Council officials' titles can be found by asking at your local CAB
office or library. For other organisations telephone them and ask who
is in charge of the subject you are interested in and what their position
is. Or contact their public relations department.

Write a letter first, explaining who you are and what you want them to do for you, for example, perhaps you want the planning department to supply facts and figures about the local population. Follow this initial contact up with a telephone call to arrange a meeting if possible.

At any meeting with officials take detailed notes and follow any promise of action on their part with a letter confirming what they promised. If the planning department has agreed to send you details of the population of the Borough by the end of the week, write to them immediately after the meeting along the lines of:

Dear Mr Ray,

We look forward to receiving the population mix figures for the Borough by Friday of this week as you promised at our meeting on October 1st.

Yours sincerely,

Sheila Brown

Note-taking is so vital that it is better to have two people at any meeting if possible. Both can take notes so that any blanks can be filled in by combining both sets of notes. Both people can ask questions so that none are forgotten.

It is always worth talking to the officials or people you are up against **in person.** An official attitude might hide a personal sympathy for your point of view, which could mean that they would be prepared to put more effort into finding acceptable official alternatives to the original plan.

EXPERTS

If you need an expert, for example an architect to look at a building about to be knocked down, and none of your friends are architects, who can you ask who won't charge you the earth? There is more help available than you think.

Lawyers
Your **local legal advice centre** will give free legal advice. To find your nearest branch get in touch with the Law Centres Federation at Duchess House, 18-19 Warren Street, London W1P 5DB (tel: 01-387 8570).

Some independent solicitors give a half hour interview for a fixed fee of £5. Ask your Citizens' Advice Bureau (CAB) for advice about where to find them.

Accountants

The **Institute of Chartered Accountants in England and Wales** (ICAEW) has twenty-two district societies and most of these have local branches or town or regional groups. Most district societies or their branches will be pleased to help find Chartered Accountants willing to act as honorary treasurers or honorary financial advisers to local groups. Allow for the fact that because of the high demand for such people, finding one can take up to six months.

Citizens' Advice Bureaux (CABs) are often supported by at least one Chartered Accountant who helps with the more difficult financial problems brought to them and most CABs have links with the Institute's district societies. If you have difficulty contacting the district societies get in touch with Alison Pidgeon, Information Officer, Practitioner Bureau, ICAEW, PO Box 433, Chartered Accountants Hall, Moorgate Place, London EC2 2BJ (tel: 01-628 7060).

For a long campaign or one which will go on for many years it might be advisable to arrange for a member to take a book-keeping course at a local Adult Education Institute (AEI).

Some of the organisations whose addresses are in the back of this book sell publications about accountancy for groups.

Architects

Someone recommended a **women's community group** of architects who were willing to survey our clinic for free because the cause was a good one and relevant to women's welfare. Ask your local women's unit or committee if anything similar is available in your area.

If you are campaigning about a listed building contact SAVE Britain's Heritage, 68 Battersea High Street, London SW11 3BX (tel: 01-228 3336) to see if they are willing to support your campaign.

Printing and photography

You might find people at your **local community centre** who would provide the expertise and training to enable you to do your own printing or photography if you are prepared to put in the work and supply the materials. They may, for example, lend cameras and train people in how to use them if you supply the film and are willing to do the developing yourself under supervision.

They may have printing machines of various sorts available and be willing to show people how to use them if the paper is paid for. You would have to provide some money and time, but this is a much cheaper method than paying professionals.

Try asking the tutor in charge of your local **Adult Education Institute** for advice on where to go. If the campaign is likely to be a long one drawn out over several years it might be worth people from the campaign taking courses in photography or screen printing at their local Adult Education Institute.

If you can find a **local community press** which is sympathetic to your cause they might teach you to use their machine or do the work for you for a reduced fee.

Of course, if you want a lot of professional help and advice over a long period you will have to be prepared to pay the proper fee. But try alternatives first. If you have a cause they believe in, experts may well help you for the sake of goodwill publicity.

More details about printing and photography are given in Chapter 7.

WHEN HELP TURNS SOUR

Every so often you will come across some piece of bureaucratic nonsense or press misreporting that makes you angry. You will want to **complain.** Should you, and if so how?

As far as the press is concerned, unless something has been said that affects the campaign severely, leave well alone. Complaints about every piece of **misreporting** would merely antagonise the press. Tell yourself that *any* publicity is good publicity. If there is a grave **error of fact**, then a polite correction is all that is required.

When somebody you are dealing with in an official capacity does something to annoy you, think about what you want to achieve. If it was a **genuine mistake,** leave it or mention it politely to the person concerned and you will quite likely get a polite apology and the mistake will be corrected.

If you have been subject to **abuse** or **gross impoliteness** from someone you are dealing with, write to their superior (there is always someone). This will usually result in speedy apology to you and sharp words to the person concerned. Very few people like to think that their subordinates are damaging the public image of the organisation by being rude to the public.

If someone has been recommended to you as helpful and is being **deliberately obstructive,** complain politely to the person who made the recommendation. He or she will be horrified as that person's behaviour will reflect on them and they will make that clear to the person concerned.

Do complain if an action taken by someone has resulted in loss of publicity or time on your part, or has adversely affected the campaign.

Chapter checklist

- Be bold in asking friends for help.
- But don't be surprised if they are unwilling to be too committed.
- Be adventurous in contacting other sources of help.
- Involve your local councillors and MP on your side.
- Approach anyone known to you who has a professional or amateur skill the campaign could use.
- List other skills needed and approach experts outside the campaign.
- Keep everyone well informed.
- Remember to acknowledge and thank all sources of help, however minor.
- Have a clear policy on when, and when not, to complain.

3
Involving the Media

No campaign can get anywhere without **publicity.** Publicity keeps the public informed about what your opponents are up to and what your campaign is doing about it. It helps to creat public sympathy for your efforts.

There are three main **media** which the campaign can use: the press, radio and television. Of these three the press is the one more likely to be used, with local radio a possibility. Television is less likely to be part of a local campaign, but should not be discounted if there is a local television station.

THE PRESS

To get good publicity a local campaign needs to be mentioned as often as possible in local newspapers, magazines, or newssheets. Most places have a local paper. Sometimes there is more than one and perhaps one or more newssheets as well.

First of all you must find out what papers are read in your community. You'll be surprised at how many **press opportunities** there are available when you look. In our area of East Dulwich and Peckham we have:

- one local newspaper
- two free newspapers
- one council newspaper
- two local society newssheets
- at least one political newssheet

Local newspapers

One of the most effective forms of publicity is to be mentioned in the **local newspaper,** that is, a newspaper with news and views about the area you live in. A local paper will be read by the people most affected by what your opponents are doing and, therefore, most interested in your campaign. Unless you are very fortunate, you won't get mentioned in the national press. But if you do, it will probably be because they have noticed a news item about the campaign in your local paper.

The local newspaper is the place to start trying to get your campaign noticed. A local paper can cover a small area, such as a village, or take news from a wide area and still consider itself local. For example, the *South London Press* covers a wide area including Southwark, Streatham, Lambeth, Wandsworth and Lewisham, but most people in East Dulwich would think of it as their local newspaper.

Often there will be more than one local paper which takes news from the same area, so your news should be sent to all the local papers to ensure full coverage. They have many interest groups competing for space in them. Although your campaign may well be of interest to the local paper it might not get the coverage you had hoped for. However if you do get mentioned, your campaign's message will get to a wide audience and the campaign will get a certain amount of local prestige.

Copies of local papers can usually be found in the local library.

Remember that not everyone buys or sees a local newspaper, so you must look for other places to send your news.

Free newspapers

If **free newspapers** are delivered in your area, use them. They are the newspapers that virtually everyone in the area will see, if not read, because the publishers aim to get them delivered to every house. This is because they depend heavily on advertising and the advertisers expect this level of distribution.

Although there is a lot of space given to advertising, these papers do carry local news. Just how much varies from paper to paper, but they all need good local stories.

If there is a free newspaper in your area you will probably get it through your door. If not, check with friends in nearby streets in case there is a gap in the delivery round. Ask friends in neighbouring areas as well in case they get a different one. Our campaign used free newspapers for Peckham, East Dulwich and Streatham/Dulwich to ensure maximum publicity.

If you don't get the free paper for an adjoining area delivered, either pick a copy up from the local office once a week or contact their subscription department and they will post it weekly for a small price.

If you want to check on which free papers cover your area, ask in your library for a copy of *A-Z of Britain's Free Newspapers and Magazines* published by the Association of Free Newspapers.

Council newspapers

Some **Councils** produce their own newspaper which is delivered free to all householders. Deliveries can be erratic, late or non-existent, so you may have to consult the copy in your libary or local advice centre.

These newspapers are mostly filled with council news and views, but you will probably have involved your local councillors already. News of your campaign can therefore be made of interest to the council paper by naming the councillors involved and saying what they are doing to support it.

Ask your local council whether its different departments produce their own newssheets. For example, we discovered that Southwark's planning department produces its own planning newssheet.

Local society newssheets

Many places have a **local society** concerned with preservation, local history, or other local issues. They often produce a newssheet or magazine for their members which can be anything from a typed sheet to a glossy magazine. These inform their members about future meetings, give details of previous ones and include information about the area.

Keep the secretary of the society and the editor of the society's newsletter informed about what you are doing. They might include a snippet about the campaign, ask you to write a short piece, or perhaps ask you to speak at one of their meetings. If the society has active members some of them may be willing to help you if they see something about the campaign in their newsletter.

Political newsletters

The **main political parties** in the area might bring out their own newsletters for their members or even everyone in a constituency, whether they are members or not. The parties not only want to press home their own point of view, but also show how interested they are in local issues.

If one of your campaign members is a member of a local political party they can probably arrange for something about the campaign to be published in their own party's paper. Try to mention any prominent local members of the party who are helping the campaign, such as councillors. But don't confine yourself to one political party or you will get accused of only representing part of the community. Keep all the political parties equally informed, even if they are not supporting your campaign.

To find out where your local branches of the major political parties are, ask at the library or the local advice centre. If they can't help, write to the national headquarters:

- Conservative and Unionist Party, 32 Smith Square, London SW1P 3HH (tel: 01-222 9000).
- Labour Party, 150 Walworth Road, London SE17 1JT (tel: 01-703 0833).
- Social and Liberal Democrats, 4 Cowley Street, London SW1P 3NB (tel: 01-222 7999).

Other possibilities

If you have a good look around your area you will find many other places to send your news. Use as many as possible, however humble they might seem. Some you could try are:

- parish or church magazines
- relevant club magazines or newsletters
- tenants' or residents' associations' newsletters
- women's groups' newsletters
- ethnic groups' newsletters
- local branches of relevant national organisations.

Ask your friends what local magazines they get.

The ethnic press

Although strictly speaking the **ethnic press** is national not local press, it is worth seeing what is sold in your area because these papers are bought by people who may not buy a local or other national newspaper.

Local issues in areas covered by these papers might appeal to the editor if he or she thinks they are relevant to their readership. Some of the ethnic press papers are:

- *Asian Herald,* Room 23, Wickham House, 10 Cleveland Way, London E1 4TR (tel: 01-790 2424).
- *Asian Times,* Tower House, 139-149 Fonthill Road, Finsbury Park, London N4 3HF (tel: 01-281 1191).
- *Caribbean Times,* Tower House, 139-149 Fonthill Road, Finsbury Park, London N4 3HF (tel: 01-281 1191).
- *The Gleaner,* Ventura House, 176-188 Acre Lane, London SW2 5UL (tel: 01-733 7014).
- *New Life,* 8/16 Coronet Street, Off Old Street, London N1 6HD (tel: 01-729 5453).
- *New Voice,* 122 Seventh Avenue, Manor Park, London E12 5JH.
- *The Voice,* 94 Bow Road, London E3 3AA (tel: 01-980 4444).
- *West Indian News,* 379-381 Brixton Road, London SW9 7DE (tel: 01-733 7052).

See what is available in your area by looking at which publications can be bought at your local newsagents. Or consult *Willings Press Guide,* published annually by British Media Publications.

Tips for dealing with the media

- Be clear in what you have to say.
- Be positive and confident.
- Be friendly but businesslike.
- Link present events to future developments.
- Be sure of your facts and able to back them up.
- Develop personal contacts wherever possible.
- Be reliable, eg in providing follow up information.
- Avoid expressing prejudice.
- Be ready to listen to advice.
- Be patient and determined.

Contacting the press by telephone

If you think that your news is interesting enough and needs to be in the papers **quickly** you can telephone. This is most useful at the beginning of a campaign when you have made your first protest. Jeannette telephoned the local paper about the threatened closure of the Amott Road Clinic as soon as she heard about it and had checked with the health authority. An item got into the next edition. It gave us a good start and we could then concentrate on sending out regular press releases.

Ask to speak to the person covering the area of news you are interested in, for example, health. Make a note of their name so that you can ask for them next time. Give your name, the campaign name, and give your news as concisely as possible. If the reporter wants to know more they will ask or arrange to telephone you later when they have checked your story.

Always keep a note of the conversation. You need to note:

- date and time of conversation
- who you are speaking to and their job on the paper, such as health correspondent
- what you said
- what they said
- any arrangements for future contact

A **personal contact** is important because it means you can get your news to someone quicker and they know what you are talking about without your having to explain it again. But don't be surprised if a completely different reporter phones you a few months later and asks you questions which you have already set out in your press releases or said many times to other reporters on the same paper. Keep calm and say it all again. The idea is to get **sympathetic coverage** by the press and not to antagonise one particular reporter.

If you don't feel confident using the telephone, either get someone else to do it or make a few notes first so that you don't forget to tell the reporter something vital.

Press releases

These form the backbone of your communication with the press and are the usual way of presenting your information to them. Start sending them out right at the beginning of the campaign and continue at **regular intervals,** perhaps once a fortnight.

For a major event, such as your MP presenting a petition to parliament, you can make the press releases more frequent by mentioning the event three times:

● the event will happen
● the event is about to happen
● the event has happened

For general information one release is enough as soon as you have the information.

Setting out a press release

Type your press releases with double spacing so that they are easy to read and the editor has room to make corrections. Try to keep all of the information on one side of a sheet of A4 paper. If you use more than one sheet the editor might lose one and in any case shorter releases are more likely to be read carefully and used. Put in the following information:

● campaign name
● contact name, address and telephone number
● the words *Press release*
● date
● heading (if needed)
● content of press release

Our press release example shows all the information included.

34 Midland Road
Whytown
Whytown 91011

BUILD WHYTOWN CROSSING MOVEMENT

PRESS RELEASE

31st May 1989

Politician adds support

Kathy Martin, prospective Member of Parliament for Whytown West, has joined other politicians supporting the campaign to provide a pelican crossing outside Whytown Primary School.

She says 'The lack of a safe crossing outside the school is a great danger, not only to the children in the school, but to all residents in the area'.

The council claims to be considering the problem. However it appears that there are no plans at present to consult people in the area.

J. Notts

A sample press release

Campaign name. This should go near the top of the press release so that the editor can see quickly who it's from and get it to the person on the paper who is dealing with your campaign. If you can get a logo designed for your letterhead to increase the visual impact, so much the better.

Contact details. You must include the name, address and telephone number of at least one person whom the editor can contact quickly if they want to know more and a deadline is close. Make sure the person you name is available most of the time, or else add an alternative contact name and number. Make sure anyone so nominated is kept up to date with the latest information about the campaign.

Press release. These words must come somewhere at the top of your press release. This tells the editor that the information is for publication and that no-one expects to get paid for it.

Date. Don't forget the date. The editor needs to know how recent the news is so that he can judge when or if to publish it.

Heading. This is not usually necessary but can be useful in letting an editor know what the contents are about. You can look forward to a heading such as 'Playground Saved!'

Contents. These should be short, clear and accurate. They should also include the 'five Ws' of journalism:

● who?
● what?
● where?
● when?
● why?

These five 'Ws' are very important and should appear in the first two paragraphs. Anything else that you want to include should go in after that. If the editor is interested in the *Why?* he can include it, or else cut it out without losing the main information.

● *Who?* Local readers like local names, so always put in the names of people who are helping you if they are known locally, such as councillors. In any case always state who is doing something or saying something of importance to the campaign. If you can quote them, with permission, do so. Quotes are always useful. When in doubt, quote yourselves. Sheila and Mary often write, 'Mrs Brown, coordinator of the 'Save Mill Street Playground Campaign, said . . .'
● *What?* This is what the press release is about. What have the *Who* in the press release been doing? Signing a petition? Arranging a meeting?
● *Where?* Has it happened somewhere locally or perhaps somewhere more central, such as Parliament?
● *When?* If it was six months ago, don't bother writing the press release. The event or information should have happened recently, be coming up in a week or two, or about to happen any minute.
● *Why?* This part is more important at the beginning of a campaign when you are trying to convince editors why they should print something about your campaign, but keep it short and accurate. It can also be added later on if the campaign has changed direction or in a first release to a new editor. But expect the *Why?* to be cut more often than anything else.

As an example of how a press release is used by a paper see our press release on page 60 and what the paper said on page 61.

Photographs

If you are holding an event and want to add a note to the picture editor about possible **photograph opportunities,** you can do so. The press should be invited to any event you organise, but we found that editors are quite capable of deciding for themselves if they wanted photographs and contacting us.

If the paper asks for a photograph of you, turn up and smile, even if they ask you to do something silly. One picture reaches more people than a short piece of writing in a local paper.

If possible wear a t-shirt with the campaign name or logo clearly visible on it. Try to get more interest into the photograph than one person standing around. How about some children, banners, people in fancy dress, balloons?

Inaccurate reporting

If you are unhappy about the **content or tone** of anything written about your campaign, do not complain. Work on the principle that any publicity is good publicity and grit your teeth, however aggravating the inaccuracy is. A long drawn out battle with the press would merely antagonise an editor and make your campaign look as it it was more worried about its image than results.

If a piece is **totally wrong,** as when we received a headline 'Clinic Saved' when it hadn't been, a polite letter of correction to the editor is all that is needed. A fair editor will print it, and in our case he headed it 'Clinic Headline Wrong'.

Patience

You'll need a lot of this when dealing with the press, especially small local newsletters which are run on a shoestring and only appear occasionally. Even if you meet the papers' deadlines, they may not have room for your piece or something more urgent may come up. It could take several weeks for your news to appear. **Don't harass the editor,** he might not print it at all if you do. In any case, campaigns are long drawn out affairs and publicity spread over many months is often more useful than a splash one week and nothing for ages.

What to write about

Something will always be happening. An MP is about to present the campaign's petition to Parliament: it's happening next week: he's done it. A local councillor has added his or her support. Local mothers are wearing campaign t-shirts. Your opponent responds to a letter from the campaign.

Save Amott Road Clinic Campaign
and Save Amott Road Clinic Project

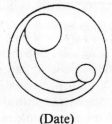

Jeannette Aspden
12 Cantfindit Road
London AB1 2CD
Tel: (01) 2345 6789

Polly Bird
34 Nosuch Place
London EF3 4GH
Tel: (01) 9876 5432

(Date)

Press Release No. 12

On Monday, February 2nd, the organisers of the Save Amott
Road Clinic Campaign, Polly Bird and Jeannette Aspden,
addressed a meeting of the East Dulwich Lunch Club at the
Copleston Centre. The meeting was attended by local health
care professionals, headteachers, social workers, librarians,
and the minister and vicar of the Copleston Centre Church.
All of these people are deeply concerned with the health and
wellbeing of local children.

Mrs Aspden made clear that, although there have been
hopeful developments, the clinic is still under threat. The
campaign will continue in its efforts to ensure that the 11,000
people served by the clinic are not deprived of this vital
community resource.

There was unanimous agreement on the importance of saving
the clinic and many offers of practical support were
forthcoming.

Jeannette Aspden   Polly Bird

What we sent the press

Mothers fight threat to clinic

LOCAL mothers have not given up their fight to save a clinic under threat of closure.

When they heard that the future of the Amott Road clinic in Peckham was threatened the mums started a campaign which snowballed rapidly.

Janet Aspden and Polly Bird rallied clinic users and the community to keep the clinic open.

Recently the two mothers addressed a meeting of the East Dulwich Lunch Club at Copelston Centre, Peckham, attended by local health care representatives, head teachers, social workers and local clergy.

Mrs Aspden said that although there had been hopeful developments the clinic was still under threat. She assured them the campaign would continue its efforts to ensure that the 11,000 people the clinic served were not left high and dry.

The clinic was due to be closed because it would cost £30,000 to do the necessary repairs.

The Health Authority wanted to temporarily rehouse the clinic in Townley Road but many mothers claimed this was too far and feared the move might be permanent.

If it cannot be repaired they would like the services transferred to a building close to the present site.

How the *Deptford & Peckham Mercury* used our press release,
19 February 1987

If you really feel that nothing is happening then it's up to you to **make sure something does.** Order some badges. Ask your MP for a quote on the latest situation, write to ask another sympathetic prominent local figure what they can do for you. Arrange a meeting with your opponents to talk through the latest developments.

Keeping going

The trick with all publicity is to **keep up the interest.** Make your press releases regular and full of news. Think of new ways of attracting the press and new ways forward for your campaign. At the point when everyone's interest is flagging, don't give up. Revive it with another news story.

Precautions
- Don't mention names of people who have asked to remain anonymous, or you'll never get information from them again.
- Don't quote without permission — although in practice you can get away with quoting anything unless it's libellous, it's best to be on the safe side.
- Don't include information given to you in confidence.
- Make sure any facts are accurate. *Check them.*

RADIO

There are now several **local radio stations** and the chances are that there is at least one broadcasting in your local area. You will find their addresses in *The Writers' and Artists' Yearbook* published annually by A & C Black & Co.

If you listen regularly to the radio you will know the names of the presenters of likely programmes and so you can send your press releases to them at the station. Otherwise send it to the editor of the relevant programme. It is not just news programmes which might be interested. There may be special slots for local groups or specialist programmes which might be interested in what your campaign is about. Don't forget women's programmes, ethnic programmes and 'phone-ins'.

If you are asked to speak on a radio programme it might be a recorded or a live interview. A **recorded interview** is less terrifying because any long pauses or offputting 'umms' from you can be edited out before the programme goes on the air. In a **live interview** you have to talk as soon as the interviewer asks you.

We were interviewed for BBC Radio *Black Londoners* programme. We prepared carefully what we wanted to say, and what we wanted *not* to say, and went along at the appointed time expecting to take part in a recorded interview. It turned out to be live. When we were interviewed we had not only to get our answers right first time, but also to give each other a fair turn at speaking.

If you are interviewed with someone else, try to make sure that it is someone you can work well with, preferably someone who has spoken with you before at meetings. For example, Mary and Sheila work well together because they often address meetings together, but John sends two of his fellow campaigners because he knows he talks too much and stops anyone else getting a word in.

But whether you are with someone or on your own, prepare carefully what you want to say. Decide what you will **not** say, which is nearly as important. This is because you may wish to keep some of the campaign's tactics a surprise for your opponents, you will want to avoid being personally abusive about people and you will not want to get sidetracked by other issues. When you have decided this run through a practice interview with a friend.

TELEVISION

Be quite clear from the start that, unless your local campaign suddenly turns into a national one, or there is some major event which will attract national attention, the **national television networks** will not be interested in your campaign.

Local television might be interested if you are planning a newsworthy and visually interesting local event which will attract a lot of people from a larger area, for example, picketting a power station, but don't rely on it. You probably know which is your local television station, but you can find the address in the phone book or *The Writers' and Artists' Yearbook*.

Send a letter about your campaign and some press cuttings to the producer or presenter of the relevant programme. Give details of any event which you think they might be interested in, and a contact address and telephone number in case they are interested. You are more likely to be successful in your approaches if your campaign links in with a current national campaign or trend. John, for instance, could link his concern about a crossing outside the school to a national road safety campaign.

Television is an outside chance, but it is always worth trying.

Keep a record

If you are lucky enough to get interviewed for radio or television, arrange for someone to **record the programme** so that you have a reference copy to quote or refer to. Otherwise you will never remember what you said. You can play it to other members of the campaign, too, if they did not hear the original broadcast.

Chapter checklist

- Survey the press opportunities in your area.
- Try to make use of each one, however small, not just the main newspapers.
- Draw up your press releases in a standard format to ensure they are both easy to handle and attractive to an editor.
- Send out a press release as soon as the campaign gets underway and keep sending them at regular intervals.
- Make sure something is always happening to keep the press interested in the campaign.
- If a group member is appointed as a contact for the media, keep them up to date with what is happening.
- Plan events which have visual impact to attract press photographers or television.
- Find out the addresses of your local radio and TV stations and the names of the producers of relevant programmes.
- Keep up to date with local programmes on radio and TV and keep the presenters informed about the campaign.
- Keep abreast of national trends and campaigns which you could link with and keep the local media informed of them.

4
Using Other Forms of Publicity

News items in the media are not the only means of publicising the campaign. There are other ways to attract the public's attention, and (even more important) to keep it. Some of these ways are:

- talks
- articles
- letters
- leaflets
- newsletters
- public meetings
- petitions
- stunts
- marches
- demonstrations
- posters
- t-shirts
- badges
- stickers

It is not good enough to organise a lot of publicity at the **beginning** of the campaign and think that that will be enough to carry you through to the end. You must **take every opportunity** to tell people what the campaign is about and what they can do to help.

People need to be kept up to date on what the campaign is doing and how it is progressing or else they will lose interest and any help given will fade away. Organisations and individuals who have given help or money need to feel that their input has been worthwhile. And there is also the need to try to get more recruits for the campaign and to enlist new people to give help or support in various ways.

You must take opportunities where you can find them, and **create them** if there are no obvious ones. Don't be afraid of saying 'Can we come and talk to your meeting?' or 'Would you be interested in an article about the campaign?'. The opposition certainly isn't going to stay in the background, so you must be bold.

If you are not certain that you can manage to give a talk, write an article or letter, or answer questions from the public, don't worry. If you cannot find someone else in the campaign who is good at doing these things, they can be learned.

TALKS

Opportunities for these will be there if you look systematically. An obvious starting point is to talk to a meeting of each political party (these are also good opportunities for asking for a whip-round afterwards). Make sure that you include all the local parties so that you appear non-aligned.

Then there are the local societies and local groups of national organisations who might be interested to hear what is going on. If you don't know anyone in the groups who can prepare the ground for you and ask for permission for you to talk, then the person to approach is the secretary of the society concerned. Write stressing the local relevance of what you will be saying and telling the secretary if you will be asking their group for help. Even if they are not likely to give you help as a group there might be individuals who would like to support you when they have heard what you have to say.

NO, DO CARRY ON, I LIKE A
GOOD HECKLER ....

If you do give a talk, **let the press know.** Even a small paragraph such as 'On Friday March 5th, John Notts, Chairman of the Build Whyfield School Crossing Movement gave a talk to the Millside Preservation Society' will be publicity for the campaign and show that you are making an effort to inform the community.

All this may seem time-consuming but part of the reason for it is to show that you do want as many people as possible to know what you are doing and to join in. Otherwise it can seem as if the campaign committee is a little clique which does not want the rest of the community involved. It is also good for campaign members to spread the word. It is all too easy to feel that things are going all right with the members you have at the present and become reluctant to encourage others to join in.

Preparing a talk

Assuming you have been asked to give a talk about the campaign, how do you set about **preparing** one?

The first thing to do is to decide what the particular group might like to know about, apart from what the campaign is for. Perhaps a local political party would want to know how the campaign is organised, what help local councillors and MPs are giving and what the campaign is going to do next. A local preservation society would probably like to know about the importance of the subject to the local community, especially if it is of historical interest, stressing the environmental aspect.

Once you have permission from the secretary to talk to a group you will be given some idea of **how long** you would be expected to talk for. If you are not told, ask so that you know how much material to prepare. Remember to allow **time for questions,** too.

The most **basic way** of writing a speech is to:

● write out what you want to say to the group word for word
● read it out to yourself to adjust the time limit
● check that all the points you want to make are there.

The danger is that it sounds stilted and boring when read out at a meeting. You will have your face buried in the paper and won't be looking at the audience. You need to keep your chin up when you are speaking so that your words carry. 'Aim at the clock at the back of the room' is sound advice.

A more effective way of planning your talk is to:

● write out your main points as headings underlined or in capitals, and then write shorter notes under each heading. Some people put these on cards, having a separate card for each main point

- stand in front of a mirror and practice giving your speech, looking at the notes only when necessary
- write out the notes briefly, as before, then don't refer to them once you have practised giving the talk. This is for the brave, but you should find that the more you practise a talk, the less you need to refer to your notes.

If two of you are giving a talk together, work out beforehand who will be making which points, otherwise you risk interrupting each other — any impression of dissension within the campaign should be avoided! After giving several talks, you will sense how to support and complement each other as speakers. It is a good idea to have two people as **joint speakers** if possible. If one dries up the other can take over and between you you should be able to answer all the questions.

Answer imaginary questions in front of a mirror. Anyone watching you will think you are quite mad, but it will give you **confidence** about replying to questions from the audience. It goes without saying that you must be quite **up to date** with all the facts and figures on the campaign.

Finally remember the audience *wants* you to do well. To them you are the expert and they would like to hear what you have to say. This may not apply to **hecklers** but any such meeting should have a good chairman who can keep order. You should keep calm and be polite.

ARTICLES

There are several local outlets for an article about your campaign. National papers are unlikely to be interested but some to try are:

- local society magazines
- local political party newsletters
- church newsletters
- newsletters of sympathetic groups.

Most group newsletters do not have much space so **submit** a short article — 500 words is about right and even this might get cut. Put in the main facts; you don't need the whole history of the campaign if the newsletter is giving information about present day activities. Your latest press releases will be a guide to what is relevant.

Type out the article in double spacing on your headed notepaper and a plain following sheet or sheets. Number them in order. Make sure that your name and address is at the top of the first sheet. You can give your article a title if you like, although this will probably be changed before it gets into print.

If you have been **asked** to write an article, make sure you know how long it is meant to be, and the date by which it is wanted (the **copy date**). It is no good sending in the article the day after the editor has sent the copy to the printers.

LETTERS

Campaigners are always asking people to write letters and everybody groans. But letters can have a **powerful effect** on authority opinion, especially if they come from people who are not running the campaign. We were told by the health authority that they had received a flood of letters which convinced them of the strength of public opinion. The actual number turned out to be six! But that was six more than usual, so even one letter has great effect. Quite apart from the possibility of changing official opinion, writing letters will bring greater publicity to the campaign.

You might write to:

- your opponents
- your MP
- councillors
- local newspapers
- local newssheets
- national society newsletters

If you write to your MP he passes your letter on to the Minister concerned with your subject, and receives a reply from that Minister which he should then relay to you. If you write directly to the same Minister you will simply get a reply from a civil servant, so it is worthwhile encouraging people to write to their MP.

Your MP might receive **information** in reply that a member of the public might not get hold of. If so, you can check this against the information you are receiving locally.

When writing to your MP it helps to say **why** you are writing. 'I am a mother of six who uses the local school.' This shows the MP and Minister that you will be affected by any decision on that particular subject, that you know something about it and gives them some measure of local opinion. Say why you are concerned about the subject of the campaign, how it will affect you, how you think it will affect the local community and ask him to let you know what he is doing about it.

You can write to your MP at the House of Commons, Westminster, London SW1A 0AA.

When in doubt about **who** to write to in any organisation, write to the person at the top. Your letter will then be passed down if necessary for someone to deal with, and you will probably get a reply more quickly than if you wrote to a department in the organisation.

For letters to the **letters page** in local papers, address the editor as 'Dear Sir'. This is not deliberately sexist but if you don't know the correct sex it is merely the accepted form. Letters to papers will mostly be informative — for example, 'I am writing to let your readers know about the formation of the Save Millfield Playground Campaign', or 'We are asking people to write to their MP' or 'There will be a Build Whyfield School Crossing Movement jumble sale' — but they will nevertheless keep the campaign in the public eye.

LEAFLETS

These can be used for telling people about **future events,** or simply for **information.** Keep the message short and readable and always put the printer's and publisher's name and address on each one in small print at the bottom. (The campaign is the publisher.)

You can get fined for giving out leaflets in the street if the police think you are causing an obstruction so the best plan is to arrange to do a door-to-door delivery using volunteers. If you are on friendly terms with a larger, more established group which is sympathetic to your aims, it is worth asking if they will deliver your leaflets with their own mailing, perhaps in return for publicity about their own activities at your meetings.

NEWSLETTERS

If the campaign is going to continue for some time then you might feel that a regular newsletter is a useful way of **keeping your supporters informed** about what is going on.

This needn't be very elaborate. Many newsletters are simple typed sheets stapled together (more about printing in Chapter 7). The simpler it is in layout and content, the better — a short address by the editor, details of forthcoming meetings and events, mention of other groups if you've promised them publicity, suggestions for what people can do to help, and so on.

Once a month is a good time span to aim at to coincide with meetings.

PUBLIC MEETINGS

There is always someone who suggests at the beginning of a campaign, 'Why don't we have a public meeting?'

If you have done your publicity well and are continuing to get publicity locally, and if you have a properly organised campaign group and have the next few months of campaigning planned, then there is little reason for calling a public meeting. And if you do organise one that is badly attended, then you could get **adverse publicity.**

- To be effective it will have to attract a large number of people — can you guarantee that?
- It will have to have interesting and publicly known local or national figures — can you arrange that?
- It will need to achieve what can't be achieved by other means — will it do that?

However, if you do decide a public meeting is vital, you will need to start your preparations well **in advance.** If you are hoping to attract a national figure to speak at it, six months is not too soon to ask them. People who are in the public eye have full diaries for months ahead. Don't be optimistic about getting someone famous to speak about a local issue. Be more realistic and invite a well-known local personality or someone connected with the subject or your campaign in an official capacity locally.

To organise a public meeting you will need to do the following:

- hire a hall and get confirmation of the booking in writing
- pay for the hire of the hall and get a receipt
- book your speakers
- arrange for a chairman of the meeting
- arrange for some members of the campaign to act as stewards at the meeting
- publicise the meeting well in advance
- collect the keys to the hall on the day or arrange to meet the caretaker, decorate the hall with posters, arrange the seating, set out relevant literature
- tidy up and lock up the hall by the arranged time after the meeting or, again, arrange to meet the caretaker.

PETITIONS

At some stage you may well want to organise a petition. If you want to present the petition to an official of an **organisation** you can arrange a deputation, or even a march to the offices to do so, but if you want to present a petition to **Parliament** then your MP must present it for you.

Organising a petition to Parliament

Contact your local MP and ask if he will be willing to present your petition to Parliament. If not, try to find another sympathetic MP nearby. There is a **special format** for a petition which needs to be followed carefully. Ask for the leaflet about petitions from the Clerk of Public Petitions in the Journal Office of the House of Commons, Westminster, London SW1A 0AA. The 'Rules concerning Public Petitions' are shown on pages 72 and 73.

HOUSE OF COMMONS

Rules concerning Public Petitions

Note—*A Member wishing to present a Petition to the House in their place should consult the Clerk of Public Petitions in the Journal Office who, after examining the Petition, will advise the Member whether or not it is a Petition which can be received and is in Order. It will then be necessary for the Member to sign the paper in the Table Office before 12 noon on the day on which he or she desires to present the Petition.*[1]

Members wishing to present Petitions on Friday should enter their names on the paper in the Table Office before the rising of the House on Thursday.

Standing Orders Nos. 119 to 123 set out the procedures of the House relative to Public Petitions.

1. A Petition may only be presented to the House by a Member of Parliament. Every Member presenting a Petition to the House must affix his or her name at the head of the first sheet.[2]

2. Every Petition offered to be presented to the House must begin with the words "To the Honourable the Commons of the United Kingdom of Great Britain and Northern Ireland in Parliament assembled ; " or with an equivalent expression.

3. Every Petition must end with a prayer setting out the general object of the Petitioner or the nature of the relief asked for, which it must be within the competence of Parliament to grant.

4. Every Petition must be written by hand not printed, lithographed or typewritten.[3]

5. Every Petition must be signed by at least one person on the sheet on which the Petition is written.[4] The first signature should be written at the foot of the Petition.

6. Every signature must be written upon the sheets upon which the Petition itself is written, and not pasted or otherwise transferred to it.[5]

7. If there are signatures on more than one sheet, the prayer only of the Petition must be repeated at the head of one side of each sheet ; but on every sheet after the first, the prayer may be reproduced in print or by other mechanical process. Signatures may be written on either side of any sheet, including that on which the Petition itself is written.[6] The " prayer " is that part of the Petition which expresses the particular object of the Petitioners (i.e. the paragraph beginning " Wherefore "), as distinguished from the allegations, circumstances or evidence set out in the first part.

8. Every person signing a Petition must write his or her address after their signatures.

9. Every Petition must be written in the English language, or be accompanied by a translation certified by the Member who shall present it.[7]

10. Every Petition must be signed by the parties whose names are appended thereto by their names or marks, and by no one else except in case of incapacity by sickness.[8]

11. The Petition of a corporation aggregate should be under its common seal, if it has one.[9]

---

[1] H.C. Deb. (1946), vol. 427, cc. 1325-6.
[2] C.J. (1833) 190, (1883) 32.
[3] C.J. (1651-59) 427, 462, (1792-3) 738-9, (1817) 156.
[4] C.J. (1817) 155.
[5] C.J. (1849) 283.
[6] C.J. (1942-43) 128.
[7] C.J. (1821-22) 172, 189.
[8] C.J. (1667-87) 369, (1688-93) 285, (1772-74) 800, (1826-27) 118, (1836) 576.
[9] C.J. (1797-98) 538-9.

[P.T.O.]

12. No letters, affidavits, or other documents, may be attached to any Petition.([10])

13. No erasures or interlineations may be made in any Petition.([11])

14. Every Petition must be respectful, decorous and temperate in its language.

15. No reference may be made to any Debate in Parliament nor to any intended Motion unless notice of such Motion stands upon the Notice Paper.([12])

16. No application may be made for any grant of public money, except with the recommendation of the Crown ; but Petitions praying for the grant of money by Bill are excluded from this rule.([13])

17. After presentation, all Petitions drawn up in accordance with the relevant Rules of the House are ordered to lie upon the Table and to be printed as a supplement to Votes and Proceedings and are transmitted by the Clerk of the House to a Minister of the Crown ; and observations made in reply by the Minister, or by any other Minister, are laid upon the Table by the Clerk of the House and ordered to be printed as a supplement to Votes and Proceedings.([14])

18. Members cannot present a Petition from themselves. While it is quite competent to any member to Petition the House, such a Petition ought to be presented by another Member. But this Rule is not to be understood to extend to cases in which Members present a Petition signed by them in their representative capacity as Chairman of a County Council or of any public incorporated body.

July, 1983.

APPENDIX

STYLE IN WHICH A PETITION TO THE HOUSE OF COMMONS SHOULD BE DRAWN UP

To the Honourable the Commons of the United Kingdom of Great Britain and Northern Ireland in Parliament assembled.

The Humble Petition of (*here insert the names of descriptions of the Petitioner or Petitioners*), Sheweth

That (*here set forth the case or circumstances to be brought to the notice of the House*).

Wherefore your Petitioner(s) pray(s) that your honourable House (*here set forth the prayer, shewing the particular object of the Petitioner or the nature of the relief asked for*).

And your Petitioner(s), as in duty bound, will ever pray, &c.

NOTE.—*The words " And your Petitioner(s), as in duty bound, will ever pray, &c." constitutes the formal ending of the Petition. After the words " &c." signatures and addresses only should follow, and no other matter should be added.*

SUMMARY OF RULES

Petitions must be written by hand and not printed, photocopied, lithographed, or typewritten. If signatures are affixed to more than one sheet, the prayer of the Petition (i.e., the paragraph beginning " Wherefore") must be repeated at the head of each sheet ; but on every sheet after the first, the prayer may be reproduced in print or by other mechanical process.

The Clerk of Public Petitions is available in the Journal Office of the House of Commons to advise informally before signatures are collected as to whether a draft petition is likely to be acceptable for presentation to the House.

---

[10] C.J. (1826) 82, (1826-27) 41, (1856) 102.
[11] C.J. (1826-27) 262, (1830-31) 748.
[12] C.J. (1822-23) 150, (1826-27) 41.
[13] S.O. No. 109.
[14] S.O. No. 122.

502955 12/84

There are certain words in the petition which must be written **exactly as stated** in the leaflet's appendix. Insert details about who you are and what you are asking for where indicated. The top copy must be **handwritten** and must not contain any mistakes. Get your MP to check the wording with the Clerk before you go to the trouble of writing it out. The top copy must be the full handwritten version. On subsequent sheets you only need the wording from 'Wherefore . . .'. With the Clerk's permission the sheets other than the top sheet can be photocopies.

The next page shows our petition heading with the obligatory words underlined.

Underneath the wording rule an equal number of lines, eg twenty, to make counting easier.

With the petition forms drawn up the next task is to collect signatures. Attach the petition forms to clipboards with a plastic cover over them in case of rain. Use biros, not pencils, for signatures because pencil will fade especially if it gets wet. Stand outside schools (with permission) or buildings connected with the campaign, go to meetings of sympathetic groups, send copies to anyone who might be able to get them filled, ask if you can leave copies in libraries, CAB offices and the like, to be collected later.

Ask people politely. Give a short explanation if required. If people refuse, be polite. It does your cause no good to be rude and argument wastes time. Do not get involved in long speeches about the campaign. The aim is to collect as many signatures as possible in the time available.

The **minimum number of signatures** required before a petition is likely to get presented to Parliament is remarkably small, about fifty. So anything you get more than that is a bonus. In fact you can probably expect to get at least a couple of hundred, unless your community is very small.

When you think you have all the signatures you need, give the petition to the MP who will present it for you in Parliament. He may have an opportunity to speak about it, but in any case it will **'lie on the table'** and that fact and whatever your MP has said will be recorded in Hansard — the Official Report of Parliamentary Debates (see page 77).

Any reply made by a Minister about it will also be recorded (see page 78).

All this is good publicity and can be exploited on the 'it *will* happen, it *is* happening, it *has* happened' pattern of press releases. Don't forget to **thank your MP** and to mention him or her by name in any subsequent press releases. Petitions give your campaign credibility and should be done fairly early on.

To the Honourable the Commons of the United Kingdom of Great Britain and Northern Ireland in Parliament assembled.

The Humble Petition of the users of Amott Road Clinic, Peckham, London SE15, and other concerned people who live and work in the area of this clinic, Sheweth

That the Amott Road Clinic, which houses a child health clinic and a Well-woman clinic, is threatened with closure by the Camberwell Health Authority and that this closure will work severe hardship on the users of this clinic and the community as a whole.

Wherefore your Petitioners pray that your honourable House will urge the Secretary of State for Social Services to direct the Camberwell Health Authority to repair the present clinic or rehouse it very close to its present site in Amott Road.

And your Petitioners, as in duty bound, will ever pray, &c.

The formal wording of a petition

STUNTS

Do be careful about stunts. It is no good thinking that it is a good idea for hundreds of people to turn out and sit in front of a tractor, if only two people actually turn up. It might have the opposite effect as far as publicity is concerned and discredit the campaign if it is seen that your supporters disappear when they are needed.

Also be careful about who your stunt is aimed at. Will it antagonise the public more than it will worry your opponents? If so, it would be better to think of less abrasive ways of gaining publicity.

Having said that, some suggestions for stunts are:

● a sit-in
● a mass balloon launch
● pavement pictures (use chalk!)
● dressing up in appropriate clothing (local anti-nuclear demonstrators dressed up in white safety suits to hand out leaflets)
● a mass walk (Sheila and Mary protested about the threatened closure of their playground by organising a mass walk with children, and toddlers in pushchairs, to the town hall).

Before organising any stunt check with the town hall for any **local regulations** you must comply with and for permission if needed. Get **police permission** too. Unless you are going to be destructive you are quite likely to get permission. The local police, if sympathetic to your cause, can be very helpful. (For details about what to tell the police when organising public events see Chapter 1.)

MARCHES

These can be a useful means of publicity if you can involve enough people. But make sure that they are **peaceful** and **well organised.** Make clear to your supporters the sort of behaviour you expect from them and arrange for several people to act as wardens and maintain discipline. If you think some people are likely to get out of control then think of another stunt. A badly behaved march will cause more trouble than it will get good publicity. If you are going ahead, get permission from the police.

DEMONSTRATIONS

Again these are only effective if well-behaved and very large. Unless there is a very good reason for staging a demonstration, don't. There are other, less antagonistic, ways of making your point. If you must go ahead, then **ask permission** from the police and arrange for **strict**

1339   *Clinic (Amott Road), Camberwell*

House of Commons

Friday 18 July 1986

The House met at half-past Nine o'clock

PRAYERS

[MR. SPEAKER *in the Chair*]

PETITION

Clinic (Amott Road), Camberwell

9.35 am

Mr. Gerald Bowden (Dulwich): I beg to ask leave to present a petition on behalf of 250 to 300 of my constituents who are concerned about the future of the clinic in Amott road which looks after well women and young children. The clinic is under threat of closure by Camberwell health authority because the fabric of the building is in a rather unsatisfactory state. The petitioners urge that Camberwell health authority should consider carefully before making any changes and that a clinic should be retained in that location.

To lie upon the Table.

discipline from your supporters. It will only take one or two people to turn it into a fight.

SUPPLEMENT TO THE VOTES AND PROCEEDINGS

Observations by the Secretary of State for Social Services on the Petition [18 *July* 1986] *from users of Amott Road Clinic, Peckham and others in the area.*

The Government fully recognise the petitioners' desire for the Amott Road Clinic to continue the provision of the services which it currently provides.

The Camberwell Health Authority is encouraged by the high esteem in which the Amott Road Clinic is held by its users and the local community. However the Amott Road Clinic buildings do present certain structural defects which would require attention if the clinic was to continue in its present location. Before committing substantial expenditure to the remedial works required the Authority is undertaking a wide-ranging survey of all Health Centres and Community Health Clinics in the District. This will correlate information on usage, condition and siting with demographic information on the local population served together with the services provided by general practitioners.

The Authority expects this survey to provide helpful information which will assist in ensuring the most effective delivery of services. Firm proposals cannot be made without the information from the survey but where these proposals involve a substantial variation in local health services the District Health Authority has agreed that they will need to be subject to formal consultation. In this way local residents will have an opportunity to comment and indeed put forward counter-proposals through their Community Health Council.

The Government do not propose to intervene in matters that are the responsibility of the Camberwell Health Authority. However if proposals are put forward that involve a substantial variation in local health services they will ensure that the necessary public consultations are fully carried out.

OTHER MEANS OF PUBLICISING THE CAMPAIGN

Posters

Posters need to be eye catching and to the point. Don't try to cram too much writing on them and make sure they can be seen from a distance. If you have a **logo** for your notepaper you could enlarge that so that the group is immediately recognisable. If you are hoping people will put them in their windows, don't make them too large. A4 size is the smallest size easily seen and A3 about the largest that will not block too much light. For walls and halls you can make posters larger if there is room.

Remember **fly-posting** is illegal.

Posters, as well as leaflets and any other printed matter such as newsletters, must have an **imprint** on them, that is, the name and address of the printer and publisher. The campaign is the publisher.

Try asking some of these to display your posters:

● friends and supporters

- libraries
- CAB
- schools
- churches
- shops
- community centres
- hospitals
- town hall committee rooms
- political party meeting rooms

T-shirts

These are excellent for publicity purposes. They are popular with the press because they **look good** in photographs and the public like to see them and possibly wear them.

Keep the design simple, perhaps the campaign logo and/or name only. Make sure that the design is positioned so that it is not distorted too much by female anatomy and is readable and visible. It is not difficult to design and produce your own and the way to do it cheaply is described in Chapter 7.

When you have some t-shirts made, contact the press. Preferably give some to prominent people such as your MP and persuade him or her to be photographed in it. In any case, try to get together two or more people wearing the t-shirts if the press want a picture.

If they are popular you could make some money for the campaign by selling some.

Badges

These are also good for publicity. They are not too difficult to design yourself and if you buy in bulk from one of the badge-making firms, such as Universal Button Co Ltd, they work out cheaper the more you buy.

Again, keep the design **simple** and the lettering **clear.** People like badges. Give some away free to supporters and sell the rest for 10p each. Chapter 7 gives details about making your own.

Stickers

The small sticky address labels that you can buy with your name and address printed on are very useful. Get some for the campaign. Use them on the backs of envelopes, on letters and as badges. They are even more useful if you can have your logo printed on them as they make **instant advertising.** Suppliers often advertise in the small ads section of national newspapers. One such firm is: Able-Label, Steepleprint Ltd, Northampton NN6 0LS (tel: 0604-810781).

Car stickers can publicise the campaign to a large number of people, whether passers-by or other road users. The plastic sort may be too expensive for a small campaign as they would need to be attractively designed, probably with a logo and memorable slogan. But the slightly bigger, gummed paper variety would probably be cheaper and would give more scope. Contact a supplier, using the Yellow Pages for advice.

Chapter checklist

- Investigate all available means of publicity, not just the main media.
- Try to arrange talks by two speakers so that they complement and cover one another.
- Keep any articles you write short and to the point — and watch copy dates.
- Keep on writing letters — to the press and to people of influence.
- Leaflets delivered door-to-door can be very effective. Look out for sympathetic organisations who already do such deliveries.
- Publicise the campaign by regular newsletter, to supporters and to influential people.
- Be very sure in advance that any public meeting you seek to arrange will be well attended and worthwhile.
- Petitions are effective, but need careful planning and preparation — and a willing MP.
- Think carefully before planning stunts, marches or demonstrations.
- Don't overlook publicity material such as posters, t-shirts, badges and stickers.

5
Using Other Organisations

A small local campaign will never have all the resources it needs for carrying on its work. It must make use of other, larger organisations which can provide practical help or information. Don't be afraid of asking other organisations for help. As long as you make use of them and do not allow your campaign to be taken over by them, then you will benefit.

You may find you need to seek **help or support** over the following:

- obtaining information
- distributing literature
- publicity
- specialist advice
- extra hands to help you
- production of or assistance with making badges, t-shirts, leaflets, and so on
- platforms for your speakers.

Once you have decided on which organisations you need to approach and what you want them to do, you can either write or telephone their headquarters. For instance, Sheila and Mary approached their local branch of the Pre-School Playgroup Association and John found out what the Fairfield Local Society could do.

In many ways it is better to **write** because you can then enclose a leaflet about the campaign and perhaps a press cutting. This gives people time to consult their colleagues. If you do **telephone**, be clear in your own mind what you want to ask and make sure you are put through to someone who can deal with your request.

Although you are asking for help, don't accept something quite **different** from what you want, just to be polite. Be sure about what help you want from an organisation and if you don't get it, say thank you and go, otherwise you will be wasting your time. **Acknowledge** any help

offered, but if none is forthcoming at least thank them for listening
because they might change their minds later. If you are offered help
and accept it it is only **polite** to continue to keep the organisation concerned informed of future progress in the campaign and to acknowledge
their help in any publicity.

If you can **give any help** to the organisation from your campaign,
do so. You might be more likely to get help yourselves if you can offer
something like publicity to the group you are asking.

Use the next page as a checklist of organisations to approach.

The following section gives brief details about a selection of organisations which might be useful to a local campaign. Some understanding
of **how an organisation operates** is necessary in order to establish
whether it can in fact help.

THE COUNCIL

When people talk about 'the council', as in 'I blame it on the council',
they are really talking about the final decision-making body of their
local authority. Local authorities are independent bodies, with paid officials (see **Departments of the council**), and with separately elected
councils. The local authorities are required, or given power by Acts
of Parliament, to carry out certain functions in their areas. Decisions
about these functions are made by the elected councils and carried out
by the paid officials.

Local authorities in England and Wales

The system of local government in England and Wales is based on:

- two tiers of local authorities in **non-metropolitan areas** — county
  councils and district councils
- a single tier in the **metropolitan areas,** and in **London** —
  metropolitan district councils and London borough councils
  respectively.

In the non-metropolitan areas of England and Wales **county councils** have responsibility over a wide area for services such as education,
major planning projects, traffic, transport, police, fire service and social
services. **District councils** are responsible for more local services such
as local planning, housing, building regulations, refuse collection and
cemeteries. County and district councils can act at the same time to
look after such things as recreation, museums and industry.

In the metropolitan areas, **metropolitan district councils** and the
London borough councils are responsible for the same things as district
and county councils, except that the fire service, police, passenger
transport, and sometimes refuse disposal are carried out by **joint bodies.**

Which organisations could help?

Type	Contact name and local address
Adult education centre	_____
Charitable organisation	_____
Commercial firm	_____
Consumers' organisation	_____
Council department	_____
Environmental organisation	_____
Ethnic organisation	_____
Financial institution	_____
International organisation with local branch	_____
Legal association	_____
Local church	_____
Local history society	_____
Local school	_____
National organisation with local branch	_____
Parent-teacher association	_____
Pre-school playgroup association	_____
Political organisation	_____
Residents' and tenants' association	_____
Sports club	_____
Student group	_____
Youth organisation	_____
Others	_____

On a more local level, **parish councils** (community councils in Wales) are elected in parishes with 200 or more electors. Parish councils look after very local issues such as allotments, community halls, recreation facilities. They must be given a chance to comment on planning applications affecting their area and can represent public opinion to local authorities and other public bodies.

Local authorities do not look after water or health services, which are the concern of independent authorities.

Scotland
In Scotland there are nine regional and three island areas, divided into 53 independent districts. The **regional authorities** carry out functions similar to the county councils in England and Wales, and the **districts** carry out more local functions.

Northern Ireland
The Northern Ireland local government system consists of **district councils.** These are responsible for many local functions and also nominate representatives to sit as members of the statutory bodies responsible for regional services such as education, libraries and social services. They represent the views of local people about other regional services, such as roads and planning, which are provided by central government departments.

Councillors
To make the necessary decisions, each local authority has a group of people called councillors who are elected by the people who live in the authority's area. Councillors are **volunteers** and receive no pay, except for an allowance and travel expenses when they attend council meetings.

A local authority area is divided into smaller sections, or **wards.** The people in these wards vote for one or more people to represent them on the council. Each local political party chooses people to stand for election in each ward. Some people are elected as **independent** councillors. As they are not tied to a party political point of view they may be willing to take risks in supporting a campaign which political councillors might be wary of.

The council meets together regularly to make major decisions. But because a full council meeting is very large, there are usually **sub-committees** of the council to deal with different aspects of the local authority's responsibility. There might be, for instance, a women's sub-committee or a housing sub-committee. At these sub-committee meetings a smaller number of councillors discusses issues of concern to that committee, reads and prepares reports for the full council and reports back to the full council with recommendations. Some councils allow sub-committees to take decisions about their own subjects; many others prefer all decisions to be ratified at a full council meeting.

Individual councillors, like MPs, sometimes hold **'surgeries'** in their ward, that is, regular sessions where members of the public can talk to them about their problems. Ask for details of surgeries at the local library.

How the council can help you

Contacting your local councillors is very useful. They can:

- **ask questions** about the subject of your campaign in their sub-committee or the main council meeting
- **propose courses of action** (put forward motions) at these meetings which, if accepted, commit the local authority to a certain course of action
- **ask to see documents** from council departments which are relevant to the subjects being discussed in their committees. The public can see the background papers from which the reports are written (unless they are confidential).

Sometimes the public are allowed to attend committee meetings and, with the chairman's permission, to speak. Find out when the subject you are interested in is being raised at any open committee meeting so that you can go along and hear what is being said. If you can't go, ask your councillor to send you a copy of the minutes of the meeting so that you can read what happened.

A good way to make sure that relevant items are not missed is to go to all committee meetings on a rota basis.

Departments of the council

The council makes decisions about what is to happen in its local authority area, but it is the duty of the **officers of the Council** to make sure that these decisions are put into action.

Don't confuse council officers with councillors. The officers are paid employees of the local authority and their role is executive, administrative and advisory. They are also neutral. Councillors are usually constrained by the wishes of their political parties, but officers must serve all political parties equally.

The council's business is performed by different departments, such as education or amenities. The officers in these departments collect and collate information for the councillors in order to provide them with the factual material on which to base their decisions. The officers might also prepare reports and make recommendations to council committees.

Do not confine yourself to talking to the department directly concerned with your campaign. It could be that another department can give you relevant information which you can refer back to the first department.

Officers of the departments can tell you who is dealing with the subject of your campaign and how to contact them. They can advise about procedure and the timetabling of reports to various committees. They can also provide you with factual information relevant to your campaign or advise you who can provide it.

WATER AUTHORITIES

There are nine regional **water authorities** in England, plus the Welsh Water Authority, which look after such things as water supply and conservation, sewage disposal, rivers, pollution, fisheries and water recreation. The water industry is about to be privatised. The address of your local water authority is in the telephone book.

DISTRICT HEALTH AUTHORITIES

These are concerned with personal health services and work closely with local education, social services and environmental health authorities. A **health authority** also has various departments which furnish its committees with information. You can find out about these departments by contacting your local health authority whose address should be in the phone book or at the library.

COMMUNITY HEALTH COUNCIL

The **consumer watchdog organisation** which keeps an eye on the local health authority is called the Community Health Council (CHC). You can contact your local CHC by asking at your library or Citizens' Advice Bureau (CAB).

Members of the CHC serve on a voluntary basis and are appointed to it by various bodies such as local authorities. The CHC holds regular meetings to discuss **local health issues.** It is possible for the public to sit in on some of these meetings and even to speak at them if the chairmen agrees. You can ask the secretary of the CHC if your campaign can be put on the agenda of a meeting and then ask to speak about it.

The CHCs are there to keep an eye on the health authority. They can protest about its plans, make recommendations, and give information and advice to the public. Bad publicity from a local CHC can make the health authority think again. If the subject of your campaign has anything to do with health in your area, such as the closure of a local hospital, then the CHC should be your first port of call for information and advice. The CHC is assisted by a full-time paid secretary with some clerical staff. If you can get the secretary on your side, you will have won an important ally.

POLITICAL PARTIES

These have already been mentioned in Chapters 3 and 4. They can give you publicity in their newsletters, and support via the MP for petitions to Parliament. They can offer you a chance to speak at their meetings and give advice on how to approach committees and their members. Councillors or MPs can write in support of your campaign or make personal approaches to people on your behalf. Use them ruthlessly but be careful about becoming **politically-biased** in your campaigning.

RESIDENTS' AND TENANTS' ASSOCIATIONS

Residents' Associations are usually made up of people in a particular area who meet to discuss matters of interest to the area, for example, local history, safety or improvements. **Tenants' Associations** are usually groups connected to a housing estate and who are concerned about how it is run. They are in contact with the council.

Both these kinds of group can help with publicity, give you a chance to speak to their groups, help with leaflet distribution (perhaps including a leaflet with their own newsletter if they are sympathetic to your cause) and by urging their individual members to write in support or to sign a petition.

THE LIBRARY

Libraries often contain more than books. Ours, for example, had a badge-making machine which they could lend to people.

A library may have a photocopying machine which is available for public use. It is also, of course, the best place to ask for local newspapers, addresses, names of local groups and so on.

The library might display your posters, or let you put a notice on a public notice board or leave your leaflets and badges for the public to take. (If they are sympathetic to your cause the librarians may even wear your badges.)

WOMEN'S GROUPS

Most sorts of campaign will be of concern to the women in your community. So contact all the local women's groups as soon as you can. You will find their addresses at the library. If you think that your campaign has **particular interest to women** you could stress this. Some women's groups do have a particular interest, for example pre-school playgroups. So if your campaign is connected to the under fives you could urge this as a reason for them to support you.

Some suggestions of groups to contact are:

● women's section of political parties
● pre-school playgroups
● ethnic women's groups
● women's support groups
● women's training workshops

You may have a **women's centre** in the town. In this case you should be able to go there (if you are a woman, of course!) and find photo-copying facilities, perhaps badge-making machines, noticeboards for posting information and details of all the local women's groups. In our town the local centre is organised by the council's **women's committee,** so contact the council first to see if such a committee exists and whether they have provided such an amenity. If your group is short of women this is something you should take steps to correct immediately.

ETHNIC GROUPS

Much of what has been said about women's groups applies also to **ethnic groups.** If your campaign group is all-white and you are not seeking support amongst the ethnic community then your campaign cannot be said to be representing the people of your area and will not be taken seriously in the community. Nationally, the ethnic media is impressively professional and broadminded and local groups are active and articulate. You will be wasting a valuable resource if you do not contact the ethnic groups in your area. You will probably find a wide range of interests covered. In our area, among many other ethnic groups, we have:

● ethnic churches
● black elderly groups
● a Cyprus association
● an Afro Asian Advisory Service
● an Islamic Cultural Centre
● an Irish in Britain Representation Group
● a Muslim Women's Association

CHURCHES

Contact the **local churches** of all denominations. Some ministers will be helpful enough to put up your poster or mention you in the church newsletter. Others might even write a letter of protest on your behalf. Any letter written by a person in authority carries more weight, so try to encourage this. Churches are broad in outlook nowadays and are concerned with the community at all sorts of levels so it is worth approaching them. It is best to write initially because ministers are very busy people.

Addresses of local churches will be in the telephone book or the *Yellow Pages* and the library or CAB will give you the addresses of other religious groups operating in the area. Don't forget the ethnic religious groups.

Be careful about some of the more unusual **cults.** Association with them can be damaging because they are not always approved of in some communities. You will have to judge for yourself whether association with certain religious groups will affect the campaign's reception in your own locality.

SCHOOLS

If your campaign affects any **local school** or **young children** in the area in general (and most campaigns will affect them or their parents), then contact the headteacher and the secretary of the PTA (Parent Teacher Association) or friends of the school group, if there is one.

You can ask for permission to collect signatures for a petition in the school playground or just outside its gates. Perhaps the school will put up your posters or let you hand out leaflets to the parents. (Don't hand anything to children because parents will quite rightly get angry.)

Teachers themselves might sign a petition if they feel your campaign is doing something worthwhile for the parents or children of their school. Ask the headteacher and the staff whether they would be willing to write as individuals or in an official capacity to support your campaign because, as mentioned above, official support impresses more easily.

There is a chance that you could be asked to talk to the **PTA** or **Friends of the School group.** You should certainly offer to do so.

If one of your campaign members has a child at any of the local schools, he or she could contact the **governors** of the school and ask that discussion of your campaign be put on the agenda for the next governors' meeting. If possible, they could ask for permission for someone from the group to address the meeting.

Schools are listed in the telephone book. Again contact by letter is best, unless a parent at the school can make personal contact with any of the staff.

OTHER LOCAL GROUPS

There are many other local groups, such as:

- local history societies
- senior citizens' groups
- pre-school and youth groups
- adult education centres

Send them an outline of your campaign's aims and offer to talk to their groups. Not all of them will be interested but you should try them all.

LOCAL BRANCHES OF NATIONAL ORGANISATIONS

Local branches of national organisations which are conducting campaigns about issues of **national concern,** such as CND (Campaign for Nuclear Disarmament) or SPUC (Society for the Protection of the Unborn Child) will not be of much use to you, except as a means of passing on information about your group. Others which have a national headquarters but which are concerned with their issues at **local level,** such as the National Childbirth Trust, are worth trying.

Don't be too hopeful about this, though. Sometimes no local groups exist and sometimes they are so wrapped up in their own cause that they cannot see how helping yours would be useful. Of course, some have neither the time nor the resources to help you. But certainly approach them. If they do want to help they have a ready-made organisation to offer publicity. Perhaps they have a meeting place you could use. They may help with the distribution and possibly production of leaflets, badges, and so on, if they have their own equipment.

If you do not know the local branch of any national organisation you are interested in, write or telephone their headquarters. You will find their addresses in the telephone book.

Resources available from national organisations

Some national organisations which either offer practical help and advice or who publish useful literature for groups are:

- National Council for Civil Liberties (NCCL), 21 Tabard Street, London SE1 4LA (tel: 01-403 3888).
  For advice about your civil rights and useful publications.

- National Council for Voluntary Organisations, 26 Bedford Square, London WC1B 3HU (tel: 01-636 4066).
  This produces useful publications.

- Services for Community Action and Tenants, 15 Micawber Street, London N1 7TB (tel: 01-253 3627), and 31 Brook Road, Sheffield S8 9FH (tel: 0742-550010).
  SCAT does not offer practical help but will give information and advice on campaigning and provide contacts in organisations who might be able to assist you.

- Directory of Social Change, 9 Mansfield Place, London NW3.
  Although aimed at charity organisations, it publishes books very useful to small groups.
- TUC (Trades Union Congress), Congress House, Great Russell Street, London WC1B 3LS (tel: 01-636 4030).
  For advice about where to go for support and information.

- Scottish Council for Voluntary Organisations, 18-19 Claremont Crescent, Edinburgh EH7 4QD (tel: 031-556 3882).
  Although not directly involved with supporting local campaigns the SCVO can provide information which would help people running a campaign and it sometimes holds relevant events and courses. Recent examples include a one-day event on lobbying and courses on using the media and writing skills.

- Wales Council for Voluntary Action, Llys Ifor, Crescent Road, Caeffili CF8 1XL (tel: 869224/869111).
  The WCVA can put organisations in touch with local support agencies, supply useful back up information such as statistics, and put groups in touch with appropriate contacts in Wales.

- SAVE Britain's Heritage, 68 Battersea High Street, London SW11 3BX (tel: 01-228 3336).
  This small charitable organisation does not give out information in an advisory capacity. Its remit is to campaign for buildings of historic or architectural value that are at risk. It can often add its weight to the fight of a local preservation group, although it cannot promise to take up every cause presented to it.

Even if the nearest local branch of a national organisation is too far away it may be worth while contacting them for at least a letter of support.

Chapter checklist

- Identify where you need help or support for the campaign.
- Track down organisations which might be able to help.
- Use your local library, Citizens' Advice Bureau, *Yellow Pages* as sources of information.
- Find out as much as possible about how organisations operate so that you know how to target your approach.
- Make your first contact by letter — don't risk antagonising busy people by an unwelcome personal approach.
- Keep your initial approach simple and direct, including brief details about the campaign — send follow-up details if necessary.
- Avoid becoming politically biased in your dealings with councillors or political parties — it will narrow the campaign's appeal.
- For the same reason, make sure you cater for all sections of the community.
- Remember that many national organisations will supply free literature or advice if unable to offer practical help.

6
Managing the Money (and Getting It!)

HAVING THE RIGHT ATTITUDE

Outsiders often think that running a local campaign does not require any money. Or not much. So did we. Once we started we soon learnt how **important** money is to any campaign.

When we started we didn't worry about finances. We thought that buying a few stamps or getting a few letters photocopied or buying a few envelopes would not cost much and could easily be spared from our housekeeping.

After three months and over £50 spent, not counting the cost of telephone calls and hours spent typing, we realised our mistake and set about asking for money.

Some people don't like to think about money in connection with a good cause like a campaign. They think that people should do it for the good of the community and be willing to pay for it out of their own pockets. But this attitude is foolish. Any member of the campaign continually forking out money is bound to resent it, even if the sums involved are small. And many people genuinely cannot afford to give even small sums, however much they support the campaign. To be looking for money at the last minute from somebody's pocket is an inefficient way of running anything. With proper book-keeping right from the start and definite sources of money, the campaign can run well, plan ahead and will inspire confidence in the public as well as its own members.

Don't underestimate how much the little things are going to cost you. Even if you donate your typing skills and telephone calls, the cost of postage alone can become enormous very quickly. A large part of your time will be spent writing to people, so you must find the money for things like paper and stamps or you will soon be tempted to cut back on this or give up.

You will need money for at least the following items:

- envelopes
- paper
- stamps
- photocopying
- typing fees (if you can't type)
- telephone calls
- files
- two cash books
- a receipt book
- an invoice book
- the printing of leaflets
- transport to meetings

Work out the prices of these things and you will quickly see that a campaign needs a reasonable amount of money just to get started, let alone continue.

Stamps will probably be your biggest expense, closely followed by **photocopying.** If you have a friend willing to use his or her computer to produce your literature you could save some photocopying expenses. Don't let the cost of a stamp or two stop you getting the campaign started, but buy a small cash book and record every expense from then on so that when you do get some money for the campaign you can claim back such personal expenses. Obtaining money or grants, especially from official sources, can take time and so, like us, you might have run up a sizeable bill before you can be repaid.

Start off on the right footing now by writing a list of everything you think you will need to spend money on for your campaign. Don't leave anything out. After you have worked out such a preliminary **budget** you can see where you can economise.

KEEPING ACCOUNTS

Many people are horrified at the prospect of having to keep financial records. The thought of adding up columns of figures or juggling with someone else's money alarms them.

Don't panic. It's really very simple and a good system is not expensive to initiate.

- Buy two small **cash books** from the local stationery shop.
- Buy one **receipt book.** (Make sure you keep receipts for these purchases because they are part of your first campaign expenses.)
- On one cash book write **'Campaign account'.**
- On the other cash book write **'Campaign petty cash'.**

BUILD WHYTOWN SCHOOL CROSSING MOVEMENT

Estimate of expenses for year ending 31st March 1989

	£ p
Stamps: eg 10 x 2nd class per week	72.80
Envelopes: 500 @ £3.50 per 100	17.50
Paper: 2 reams @ £4.00 per ream	8.00
Flimsy paper: 2 reams @ £2 per ream	4.00
Carbon paper	2.00
Photocopies: 500 at max. of 10p each	50.00
Telephone calls	40.00
Box files: 3 @ £4.50 each	13.50
Card files: 10 @ 20p each	2.00
Plastic files: 10 @ 20p each	2.00
Notebooks	5.00
Address stickers	5.00
Transport to meetings with officials	20.00
Hire of hall for public meeting	50.00
Sundries, eg pens, glue, Tippex etc	10.00
Cash and invoice books	5.00
Printing 200 leaflets	25.00
Badges:. 500	65.00
	396.80

A sample budget

● Open your campaign account book up to the first double page.
On top of the left hand page write **'Incoming money'**, at the top
of the right hand page write **'Outgoing money'**.

You are now ready to start.

On the **left hand page,** under 'Incoming money', write down the date
in the left hand column when you received any money, for example,
a donation. Write down who gave you the money next to it, and in
the cash columns write down how much.

On the **right hand page,** under 'Outgoing money', write down the
date you paid any money out (for example for the cash books), what
the payment was for, and in the cash column write down how much
you paid. Then put the receipts for what you bought in an envelope
marked **'campaign receipts'**.

Every time the campaign receives some money or pays money out
record it straightaway on the appropriate page and write out a **receipt**
for the person giving you the money.

An example of an account page is shown below.

DATE	INCOMING MONEY	£	P	DATE	OUTGOING MONEY	£	P
19 Jun	Collection	31	77	19 Jun	Petty cash	31	77
3 Dec	Grant	300	00	23 Jun	Petty cash	10	00
4 Feb	Donation from Mr. Jones.	5	00	10 Jul	Mrs Brown (repayment for paper)	15	35
				4 Aug	Badges (Button Co)	65	20
				8 Sep	Stickers (Marprint)	6	50
				9 Sep.	Repayment to Mrs. Turner (stationery)	4	23
				11 Oct	Stationery (Smiths)	42	10
				16 Nov	Petty cash	20	00

A page from a campaign's main account book

When you need some cash in hand for things like stamps write the
date, then **'petty cash'** and the amount you are taking for petty cash
on the 'Outgoing' page of your account book. In your **petty cash
book** the same amount will be recorded under 'Incoming money'. Then any
petty cash you spend is recorded under the 'Outgoing money' in the
petty cash book and the receipts kept in the same way as for the main
account book. That way you have a complete record of every money
transaction the campaign makes and anyone who wants to can see that
you haven't run off to the Bahamas with the money!

DATE	INCOMING MONEY	£	P	DATE	OUTGOING MONEY	£	P
19 Jun	Collection	31	77	23 Jun	Stamps	3	00
23 Jun	Petty cash	10	00	"	Photocopies	11	96
				"	Tippex	—	28
				24 Jun	Envelopes	1	77
				"	Photocopies	2	44
				7 July	Photocopies	—	80
				27 July	Photocopies	1	61
				12 Aug	Stationery	1	72
				2 Sep	Photocopies	4	20
				15 Sep	Photocopies	1	00
				25 Sep	Stamps	1	20
				17 Oct	Envelopes	1	27

A page from a campaign's petty cash book

Bank account

When you have some money and the campaign is on an official footing you will need to open a bank account. For this **two officials** of the campaign (usually the chairman and treasurer — see page 22) must go to the chosen bank and open a campaign account. Any official account will require two signatures, so make sure the two people who will have to sign the cheques will find it easy to get in touch with each other.

The bank will also want to have a copy of the campaign's **constitution** so that they can be sure that any money is being efficiently looked after.

Banks usually levy **bank charges** on official accounts so you will have to allow for these in your budgeting. But it is worthwhile asking the manager if the bank will waive charges for such a good cause. Our bank did.

After a week or two the campaign will receive **cheque books** bearing the campaign name and from then on will receive regular **statements.** These must be kept carefully. The one snag is that you will not usually get a cheque card and so if you pay by cheque a shop may want to make sure the cheque has gone through the bank (been cleared) before supplying you. This usually takes three days. If you don't want to wait you will have to cash a cheque and then pay the shop.

On the cheque book stubs record not only the amount paid out, but also to whom and for what as a double check on your cash books.

Annual accounts

The whole point of keeping accounts is to make sure at the end of the financial year that the amount you have spent and the amount remaining in your bank account and petty cash tin are the same as the amounts shown in your account books.

For small campaigns, where the funding is not large or is mainly from donations, it may be enough for the treasurer to produce an end of year accounts statement, together with the account books and the bank statements at the Annual General Meeting for inspection. But if you are receiving funding of any amount from an outside organisation then you will probably be asked to provide **audited accounts.**

It may be a condition of your grant that audited accounts be provided at your expense. If so, allow for the cost of asking an **accountant** (see page 48) to do this before you dispose of any money. If you have a friend who is a practising or retired accountant so much the better. An accountant will want to see your end of year accounts, as well as all the books, statements, cheque books, receipts, and so on, relating to the campaign finances. He or she will then check that the details as recorded are correct and write a **statement** officially confirming this.

Sometimes, if a grant is small, you may only be asked to send in **your own accounts** with all the receipts to prove that you have spent such money. You should then write out the accounts, with everything added up and the totals recorded, and send that in with the receipts.

SOURCES OF MONEY

You will have thought of some sources of money. Typical ones include:

- donations
- subscriptions
- selling of campaign goods, such as t-shirts
- a jumble sale
- entry fees to events
- a grant
- a whip-round at a meeting
- sponsored events.

Donations

When you first start campaigning you will probably find that most of your money comes from this source. The amounts will in all likelihood be very small, but do not despise them. And don't fail to **record** them and give a receipt if required. People want to be sure that their money is being used for the campaign so you must be able to show in your accounts that you received it.

BUILD WHYTOWN SCHOOL CROSSING MOVEMENT

Statement of accounts for year ending 31 March 1989

RECEIPTS

	£ p
Donations after ward meeting	31.77
Grant from XYZ Fund	350.00
Subscriptions	21.50
Sale of badges	14.70
	417.97

PAYMENTS

	£ p
Stamps	55.87
Photocopies	68.20
Stationery	44.58
Telephone calls	37.41
Stickers	3.90
Badges	66.70
Leaflets	32.00
Hire of hall	45.00
Audit fee	25.00
Transport	15.70
Cash in hand as at 31 March 1989	3.61
Cash in bank as at 31 March 1989	20.00
	417.97

I have examined the books and financial records of the Build Whytown School Crossing Movement and certify that the above accounts represent a true and fair view of the finances of the Movement for the year ending 31 March 1989.

(signed) Ledger & Greysuit
          Accountants

Sample audited accounts

You could try asking shops, schools and other organisations to see if they might give donations.

Subscriptions
Think carefully about these. In a large campaign people expect to be asked for a pound or two each year to help with the campaign's running expenses. In a small local campaign, where the time limit is not known, people may not be so willing to give regularly. If you do ask for a subscription then **make it small,** perhaps no more than 50p so that no-one feels too put upon by it.

Selling campaign goods
This source of income means you must have something to sell that people **want to buy.** T-shirts are an obvious example of this and people are often willing to pay out for a nicely printed t-shirt which they feel they could wear even when the campaign is over.

Other things that could be sold are:

- sweatshirts
- badges
- stickers
- newsletter.

Try to get goods printed or made cheaply or by friends so that you can keep the prices low but still make a profit. See Chapter 7 on self-help options.

Jumble sales

These are tiresome to organise and run but they do **make money.** If
you are really broke try one. Try to get the hall donated free and charge
10p admission to the sale. If you have to pay a fee for the hall remember
that you need to make at least that amount to break even. Teas and
refreshments are very popular at jumble sales so do try to provide them.

Entrance fees

As at jumble sales, admission could be charged for some events, but
these would have to be worth paying for. If you organised a small con-
cert you could **charge admission,** or perhaps hold a party where admission fees would go into the campaign funds. But be careful — there
are laws about charging admission to a party where alcohol is available.

Events like these take a lot of hard work to organise so make sure
that people are willing to see it through before you go ahead.

Grants

A grant is an ideal source of funds if you can get one. Try the council
first.

Another source might be one of the benefactors listed in *A Guide
to the Major Grant Making Trusts,* edited by Luke FitzHerbert and
Michael Eastwood. This lists various grant-giving bodies with a brief
indication of the sort of causes they donate to. A letter to some of those
who look as if they might be sympathetic to your sort of campaign will
be worth a try. Sheila and Mary wrote the letter on page 102.

In order to get a grant you might have to fill in a form giving details
of what your campaign is about and giving information about your
officers and bank account. Different organisations will have different
forms and there may well be variations on the forms for other types
of grant. You will have to make it clear whether you want a grant every
year or just the once. It is sensible to assume that you will only be campaigning for a short time and ask for a one-off grant. Then if you are
successful and the campaign needs to continue for more than a year,
you can reapply with proof that you spent the previous grant wisely.

One example of a grant form is shown in the appendix starting on
page 127. It looks complicated, as you can see from the pages reproduced, but in fact it is straightforward enough taken step by step.

Don't be afraid to ask the grant-giving body for advice on filling
in the form. We were given help in answering the questions to the maximum effect and in making sure that our replies would satisfy the requirements of the council's lawyers. Detailed notes came with the form
about the kind of information needed in order to answer each question satisfactorily. Obviously, your grant form might be different but

SAVE MILL STREET PLAYGROUND CAMPAIGN

7 Midfield Road   19 Barton Close
Fairfield   Fairfield
tel: Fairfield 1234   tel: Fairfield 5678
                                              14th June 1989

The Director
The Charles Wednesday Foundation
Charles House
London

Dear Sir,
    We understand that your organisation has a particular
interest in child-based community groups. Our campaign to
save our playground may therefore be of interest to you.
    We are a group of local parents who are trying to stop the
closure of our local playground in Fairfield.
    The playground is well-equipped and maintained, and
widely used by local children. The nearest alternative
playground is three miles away across a main road.
    The Council plans to close the playground to save money.
We have been actively campaigning for six months to change
their minds.
    If you feel able to make a grant towards our campaign, we
would be very grateful. Your organisation would, of course,
be given due credit.
    Our sources of money so far have been subscriptions and
donations. We would be pleased to show you our accounts
and to answer any questions about the campaign that you
might wish to ask.
    We can be contacted at either of the above addresses.

                    Yours faithfully

                Sheila Smith (coordinator)
                Mary Brown (treasurer)

An approach to a grant-giving body

this will give you some idea of what to expect. If the form seems long, remember that an organisation will know nothing about you except what you yourself tell them so they have to ask detailed questions before they part with any money.

You will need a **constitution** too. Again, go back to the grant-giving body. They may be able, as Southwark did, to give you a sample constitution on which to model yours. If so, follow it as closely as possible and again ask for help if you are not sure what to put. The sample constitution we followed is shown on page 104 (our own constitution has already been shown in Chapter 1, page 27).

If you are given any major financial aid, you must **acknowledge** this in any publicity handouts. This is part of the payment you make for the grant and, in any case, it is only courtesy to record your appreciation. The receipt of a grant will of course make a press release of its own (see p.105). Send the grant-giving body information about your continuing activities so that they can see how the money is being spent and that their name has been mentioned.

Like any other money received, a grant **must be recorded** in your cash books as well as being paid into the bank.

Whip-rounds
These are highly recommended. If you give a talk to any group of people ask the chairman **beforehand** whether you can have a whip-round afterwards. Experience has shown that people give much more this way than if they are asked for a donation without any warning. They tend to give whatever loose change they have in their pockets, and sometimes more.

Don't be shy about asking. Everyone does it and you need all the money you can get. Occasional whip-rounds at your own meetings, too, will bring in the money for small projects, but don't try this too often.

Sponsored events
These are an excellent way of making money. Think of something you could do, such as running round a field or swimming lengths of the swimming pool, then ask people to sponsor you for so much per lap or length.

People seem to find this an acceptable way of giving money and virtually anything sensible or silly will do, from a sponsored slim to a sponsored bed-push from Land's End to John O'Groats.

CONSTITUTION

NAME:

    The group will be known as the 'Southwark Women's Group'.

AIMS & OBJECTIVES:

    The aim of Southwark Women's Group is to provide a forum for women in Southwark to meet together and discuss issues of concern to women in the Borough. To further these aims, the group may put on events, publish information, raise funds and undertake any other lawful activity relevant to aims of the organisation as may be decided by the group from time-to-time.

MEMBERSHIP:

    Membership of the group is open to women living or working in Southwark who are concerned to further the interest of women in the Borough. Applicants for membership will be approved by the group at a general meeting.

STANDING ORDERS:

1. Members of Southwark Women's Group shall constitute the management committee of the organisation.
2. The group shall elect a Secretary and Treasurer each year at the Annual General Meeting.
3. The group will hold a general meeting at least once a month. Members will be notified of the time and place of meetings, and the agenda, at least 7 days before the meeting.
4. No decision can be taken at any general meeting of the group unless five members are present.
5. Between meetings, the Treasurer and Secretary can make decisions which cannot be deferred until a general meeting is called. Any such decision will be ratified at the next general meeting.

ANNUAL GENERAL MEETING:

    An Annual General Meeting shall be held each year within 3 months of the end of the financial year. This meeting will:

(a) review the work of the group;
(b) approve audited accounts;
(c) elect a Treasurer & Secretary;
(d) nominate auditors for the following year.

A model constitution (Used by permission of the Southwark Women's Equality Unit)

Cash boost aims to help save clinic

A GRANT of £300 from the women's committee of Southwark Council is the latest gesture of support for the Save Amott Road Clinic Campaign in Peckham.

The campaign has been active since last March and aims to stop the closure of the children's clinic which is due for urgent building repairs.

Jeanette Aspden and Polly Bird are spearheading the campaign which has recently won the centre a reprieve until April.

Clinic users have been backed in their campaign by local councillors Jessica Wanamaker and John McTernan as well as gaining the unanimous support of Southwark Council and the local community.

The grant from the women's committee will help towards publicity and administration expenses which have been borne by the campaigners until now.

A zoning plan which is intended as an overview of health care provisions in Camberwell is currently being carried out by Camberwell District Health Authority.

The results of this plan are expected to be vital in deciding the fate of the Amott Road Clinic and could mean that health care provisions are upgraded.

The result of a press release about grant aid (*Peckham & Dulwich Comet,* 9 January 1987)

Chapter checklist

- Have the right approach to finance from the outset.
- Don't underestimate how much you will need to start — draw up a budget.
- Keep proper financial records right from the beginning — they need not be complicated.
- Devise ways of raising funds suitable to your campaign.
- Be scrupulous in recording money received and giving receipts.
- If applying for a grant, don't hesitate to ask for help in filling in the application form.
- You may need to supply copies of your constitution and then your audited accounts to a grant-giving body.
- Seek help from an accountant if you have to supply audited accounts.

7
Stretching the Money

Local campaigns do not on the whole have much money, and what they do have they need to spend sparingly and to the best advantage. It is therefore only good sense to look for the cheapest ways of producing or obtaining any leaflets, posters, badges, t-shirts, letters, and so on, for the campaign's needs.

The easiest way to reduce costs is to know somebody who has access to the necessary equipment or raw materials and who is willing to produce items for nothing or at cost because they want to help. In this case, don't be shy about asking them for help and asking how cheaply they can do the work. Ask where it will do the most good and hold everyone to any promise of help made.

If you don't know of an obliging friend, are you forced to pay expensive commercial prices? No. This section will tell you how to obtain things cheaply or how to produce your own material.

PRINTING

For a few letters or leaflets photocopies will not be too expensive. In your local **photocopy shop** or **library** the price is usually around 10p per sheet. In photocopy shops the price per copy goes down the more copies you want, which is useful if you need 50-100 copies. There may be a **community centre** or **women's centre** in your town which provides copies below commercial prices. If so, see if you can take advantage of this. Ask at your library or town hall.

But the cost of these cheaper methods mounts up too, and eventually you will need to make hundreds of copies of leaflets or letters. Photocopying then becomes too expensive.

The next cheapest method is the old school-type stencil machine or **duplicator.** This involves typing the copy onto a special waxed sheet (a stencil). The type pierces the stencil to make a master. The stencil is fixed around the drum of the duplicator which is fed with ink. The

107

machine forces the ink through the stencil onto the paper. Although later machines have been greatly improved this process can still be messy and amateurish-looking. With good quality stencils it is all right for about 250-500 copies, before the stencil gets clogged and needs renewing, but this should be adequate for a campaign newssheet.

For printing large quantities **local printers** are worth a try. They might be willing to cut their prices a bit for a good cause. Many printers nowadays use offset litho technique which means that printing is comparatively cheap and usually well within the price range of a local campaign.

With the right contacts you might even find a **local company or organisation** that has its own printing facilities which they might let you use. Or they might allow the printing to be done cheaply for you.

Ask around to see if there is a **local resource centre** in your area. These are places where people from the community are encouraged to learn skills, such as photography and printing, and to use those skills to study their community. There may well be print facilities available there. If so, you would be taught how to use the printing machines and then do the printing yourselves under supervision. This is a good way of getting printing done cheaply if any members can spare the time to learn the processes involved.

Computers

If you are lucky enough to have a member who owns one and is willing to put it to use for the campaign, a computer is a very useful tool.

You can type a letter or press release onto a computer and it will **print out** one or more copies. You can make as many copies as you need and then some more later if you need extra, because the information can be **stored on disc.** A daisy-wheel printer will give electric-typewriter quality type but the dot matrix variety is perfectly adequate for copies of letters.

You will probably offer to pay for the paper and ribbon and, if necessary, typing time, but this is not necessarily expensive for the ease and efficiency of computer print outs.

Letters

Letters warrant a separate heading, even though the printing techniques have been mentioned above, because their overall appearance will benefit from being designed as well as nicely produced.

It is of definite advantage to a local campaign to devise some kind of **letterhead** which will distinguish your letters from the mass of other letters going to whatever authority you are dealing with. An authority's attitude to an 'official' campaign is much more forthcoming than to just anyone who writes in. If they can spot straight away that a letter is 'official' they will give it more serious attention. (Of course they may become so fed up with you that the sight of your letterhead means the letter goes straight in the bin, but let's for the moment be optimistic!)

You could just have the name of your campaign as your letterhead, with the campaign's contact name and address. If you are using a printer he will typeset this for you, or you can make up a master yourself using **Letraset.** But if you can devise a **logo** so much the better. Ours was designed for us and it is simple but clear (see below).

Save Amott Road Clinic Campaign

Jeannette Aspden
12 Cantfindit Road
London AB1 2CD
Tel: (01) 2345 6789

Polly Bird
34 Nosuch Place
London EF3 4GH
Tel: (01) 9876 5432

An example of a printed letterhead with logo

When designing a logo you need to decide:

- What is the one thing that symbolises our campaign? (For Sheila and Mary 's playground campaign it might be a swing or a roundabout, for John's crossing, a pelican light.)
- Do we need lettering in the form of initials, our campaign name or a slogan?
- What shape should it be?
- Do we need different designs for letterheads and t-shirts?
- Will the design be clear when reduced or enlarged?
- Do we need colours in the design?

You need someone who can draw to produce the logo design actual size in black indian ink on white cartridge paper or card. Stick it in the correct position on the master letterhead to provide the necessary artwork. Then take the artwork to your printer who will be able to produce perfect copies to use as letterheads.

Letterhead designs printed on narrower strips can be used as compliment slips, thank you slips or invitation slips.

If you don't know anyone who admits to artistic talent why not ask the local art college or a school? They might like to design a letterhead or logo for you as a project in return for recognition in some way.

NEWSSHEETS

These can be produced inexpensively on a duplicator or computer, or be photocopied sheets if numbers are small enough. They need not be more elaborate than a **single typed sheet** on headed paper. If more sheets are needed they can be sorted and stapled in the right order by volunteers, again keeping costs down.

BADGES

Everyone loves badges, so do get some made. You will need several hundred badges to make it worthwhile because you will want to hand them out or sell them to as many people as possible. They are one of the most effective forms of publicity.

It is possible to **make your own** by borrowing a badge-making machine from your local library, youth centre, resource centre, or another local organisation that has one. If you borrow one of these it will take time and patience to produce the badges. Each design will have to be drawn or printed on circles of paper of the right size. Several can be drawn on one sheet and then photocopied. Each circle is cut out separately, covered with a protective transparent disc and then punched into the mould. Then the pin has to be attached to each one by hand. It can be done but if you haven't got the time or need the badges quickly, then for a few pence more per badge you can get the job done professionally. If you want about 50-100 badges try doing the job yourself, otherwise use a supplier.

There are several **badge-making firms** around. The cost per badge goes down the more you order and also depends on the size of the badge and what colours you use. As an example, we ordered five hundred 38mm badges in our design in one colour (black) on white.

Badge for the Save Amott Road Clinic Campaign

This cost us £66.70 including VAT and therefore worked out at about 13p per badge. If we had done it ourselves it might have been a bit cheaper, but not enough to make it worth the time it would have taken.

A badge-making firm you could try is the Universal Button Co. Ltd, 1-9 Birbeck Street, Bethnal Green, London E2 6JZ (tel: 01-739 5750 or 01-739 8309).

A large proportion of the cost of getting the work done commercially is for preparing the photo-plate for the design. If you ask the in-house designer to make sense of a rough sketch it will cost more, but if you can produce yourself, as we did, an actual size badge design ready for reproduction then the cost goes down.

It is perfectly possible to **design** a badge yourself. Use black indian ink and Letraset lettering and draw the design actual size on cartridge paper or card. Allow a few extra millimetres around the edge for turning in.

T-SHIRTS

These are also very popular with supporters and can be **printed yourself**. The main cost will be in the t-shirts. You could ask each person to bring one and then arrange for someone to put the design on, or buy in bulk yourself. Your local market is probably a good place to look for cheap t-shirts. You can get them for under £2 each if you look around.

If you do buy some make them large rather than small. Cotton t-shirts are the cheapest sort but they invariably shrink. If you buy the small sizes then when they've shrunk after one wash no-one will wear them, except children. Large sizes allow for shrinkage and will fit more people. Try to get t-shirts in pale colours so that any design will show up.

If you only want to produce one or two, perhaps for a photo session, then you can use fabric crayons available at art shops and large stores. Stretch the t-shirt over some smooth board and simply write and draw on your design. The shirt is then removed from the board and ironed on the wrong side to fix the crayoning.

Some important points to note:

- Beware of where you put the design so that it doesn't disappear round the back of the garment or become unreadable over the bust!
- Make the design about a foot square and place it fairly centrally. The campaign logo would be ideal if you can draw it.
- Although crayons are supposed to be fast when ironed, they can smudge and run a bit, so keep these t-shirts away from anything else.
- Fabric paints are also available and with these too you can paint the design on and fix it with an iron. These should be washable.

If you like the idea of individuality you could organise a campaign 't-shirt paint and draw-in' where everyone brings their own t-shirt and produces their own version of the campaign logo!

All this is fine if the t-shirts are only for your own campaign members. But if you want to sell them to the general public or give them to people like councillors for publicity then they need to be more professionally produced.

Screen printing is one way of doing this. It is a way of printing a stencil design onto paper or material. If done well the results are very clear and smart. You can buy screen printing outfits at craft shops or make your own. See *The Alternative Printing Handbook* by Chris Treweek and Jonathan Zeitlyn (Penguin, 1983) for ideas.

You might have a member who has done some screen printing and would be willing to print the shirts you supply if someone else does the design. If the campaign is likely to go on for some time, it might be worthwhile for a member to take a course in screen printing at a local adult education class.

Again the problem of design crops up. Ask your local art college if they could use the chance to design and print your t-shirts (or, indeed, posters or anything else) if you provide the materials. You might be able to persuade them that it would be good practical experience for their students and good publicity for the college (although you would need to make it clear in your own publicity that the college does not necessarily support the campaign).

If you do approach someone else to do the designing and/or printing for you make sure that you **keep control** of what the finished result will be like. Whether you are paying them or not, remember *you* are in charge. A local college agreed to help a campaign by designing and printing some t-shirts. The campaign was to supply the t-shirts and discuss the project with the students. In fact, before there was opportunity to do this, the campaign was suddenly presented with over a dozen printed t-shirts. Not only had it not provided the shirts, it had not seen the design beforehand — and the name of the campaign was incorrectly spelt making the shirts useless! Be warned by this and oversee the design and printing closely. Otherwise everyone's time and money will be wasted.

Commercially printed t-shirts with a one colour design can cost anything from about £2.60 to £4.00 per t-shirt for a minimum order of a dozen. The more you buy, the lower the cost of each shirt will be. One reasonably priced firm is: Magnum Shirts, Rose House, Dunsfold Road, Loxhill, Godalming, Surrey GU8 4BJ (tel: (Hascombe) 048362 481).

POSTERS

In many ways the problems are similar to those of producing the t-shirts. Screen printing is a good way of producing **multiple copies** and local students might help with design and/or printing if you don't have any members who could do it.

For **one or two** large posters (perhaps for display on the walls of a hall) you could draw out the design yourself. Lettering should be large enough to see and the information be clear and to the point. Lettering can be done with a broad pen or traced from a book of alphabets. Try to be neat and make the letters large enough to be read at a distance. But don't panic about the odd splodge. The main thing is to advertise the event the poster is for.

For display in windows the poster should be smaller. Some photocopiers will reduce fairly large designs to A3 or A4 size. A4 (standard typing paper size) is surprisingly visible in a window without obscuring the view or blocking too much light. Our poster on page 114 was produced A4 size.

Smaller posters can be produced by using a card stencil or lino cut prints. For lino prints, buy special lino from art shops and borrow some lino-cutting tools from a school. Cut away any lino where you don't want anything printed, remembering to reverse any lettering. Put some printing ink on a piece of glass and roll a rubber roller over it and then onto the lino. Put a piece of paper onto the lino and rub all over it with the back of a spoon to print the design. You can produce hundreds of copies from one lino-cut if you have the time.

A good book on graphic design in general is *Do-it-Yourself Graphic Design* edited by John Laing, and published by Ebury Press (1984).

PHOTOGRAPHS

As part of campaign publicity you may want to send out photographs, perhaps to illustrate a press release or to send with an article to a magazine or newspaper. To take photographs yourself is obviously cheaper than hiring a photographer.

The most usual equipment is an SLR (single lens reflex) camera with a black and white film. If you are photographing people, their faces need to be clear and there should be little unnecessary background, so you will need skill in taking close-ups.

Developing and printing can be done by an amateur with his own darkroom or you could borrow a darkroom at a resource centre or Adult Education Institute centre if necessary. There are also cheap and fast processing and printing services offered in the small ads sections of magazines like *What Camera?* and *Amateur Photographer*.

Save Amott Road Clinic Campaign

12 Cantfindit Road
London AB1 2CD
Tel: 2345 6789

34 Nosuch Place
London EF3 4GH
Tel: 9876 5432

SAVE THE AMOTT ROAD CLINIC

The Health Authority is Planning to Close
Our Local Child Health Clinic.
Yours May be Next.
Dont Let Them do it.

Please Put This Notice in Your Window and Write to:

Maggie Mansell Secretary
Community Health Council
75 Denmark Hill SE5 8RS

Telephone 703 9498

and Gerald Bowden MP
House of Commons
SW1A OAA

Bear in mind how the press likes photos to be supplied. They should be black and white, unbordered, glossy, and 8″ by 10″. Captions giving the names, date and event should be typed on sticky labels and attached to the back of the photos with the name and address of the photographer and the campaign.

If there is no-one in the campaign who can produce photos to a suitable standard for press use then it is possible to take a course in photography, either at adult education classes or at a resource centre. But think carefully whether you actually need to take photographs yourself. If you are staging an event that the press might be interested in tell them, and, if it as newsworthy as you think, they will send their own photographer. If you keep the press fully informed about the campaign's progress and events they will be able to decide for themselves whether a photograph is needed.

GREETINGS CARDS

Christmas cards are a good way to remind people about your campaign and this can be quite cheaply done if you produce your own. You can either draw your own design with indian ink or use lino cuts. If you need to send out more than a few you can get them printed at your local printer.

A simple one-colour line design on coloured card will not be expensive. Why not use your logo as we did on our campaign Christmas card (see page 116)? As an example of cost, our printer charged us £42 for 250 cards on A6 sheets, folded and with envelopes. Don't ask for wording inside because that is much more expensive. If someone can draw an actual size design as artwork for the printer to use that will save money.

Chapter checklist

- Campaign finances will need to be used sparingly.
- Don't commit the campaign to any expense before you have considered alternative ways of getting what you want.
- Find out which members have a talent which could be used, or a contact to another source of help.
- Investigate sources of help in your community.
- Keep an up-to-date register of the services they offer, or equipment or facilities you could use.
- Find out what courses are held locally which might be of use to the campaign.
- Check whether your local school or college would be able to help in any way as part of a project or coursework.

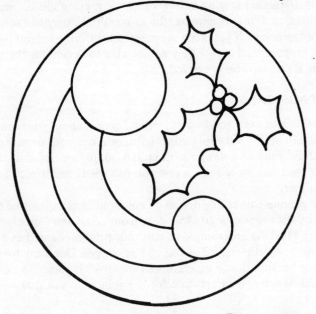

Christmas card for the Save Amott Road Clinic Campaign

- Check your library for useful books of guidance and step-by-step advice.
- When all else fails, have a go yourselves.
- Keep control over the design and finished appearance of all campaign products.

8
Now It's Over

WHEN TO STOP

All campaigns come to an end. Some end sooner than others. But how can you tell when to stop?

Winning

The obvious ending to a campaign is whenever you have **achieved** your main objective, whether to save a playground or get a new crossing built.

Don't be tempted to add 'just a bit more' to what you originally wanted to do. If the campaign was set up to stop a listed building being demolished, don't then go on to extend it to include asking for its garden to be turned into a public park. When the building has been saved, stop. Then, if you want to, start a new, separate campaign about the garden. If you add too many bits and pieces, the campaign will never end and your support will be weakened because nobody will be sure what the campaign really stands for. Sheila and Mary won their campaign because the playground was saved. The Council decided to save money by making cuts somewhere else. Both women would like to see new toilets on the site, but that must be a separate campaign.

The active part of the Save Amott Road Clinic Campaign ended when the health authority agreed that the clinic services should stay (see page 119).

Losing

Of course, the campaign might end because **you have lost.** For example, John did not get the pelican crossing he wanted outside Whytown Primary School. In this case he might feel that campaigning about re-routing traffic is worthwhile, but again, he must make it a separate campaign.

Child clinic is saved by mums

OVER 18 months of campaigning by local mothers has saved a threatened children's clinic at Amott Road.

Campaign organisers Jeannette Aspden and Polly Bird enlisted the help of MPs from all three major parties and won all-party support from local councillors in their fight against Camberwell Health Authority.

The health authority has now published a draft report recommending that the clinic should stay and that it is well used.

"At first they said not enough people used the clinic, but their own current study shows that more than 2,250 children are seen at that clinic," said Ms Aspden.

The existing clinic is damaged by subsidence and could be unsafe. Health authority suggestions now include underpinning the building and using pre-fab accommodation on a nearby site.

Ms Aspden added: "I am delighted."

Peckham & Dulwich Comet, 25 September 1987

Giving up

A more debatable situation arises when your opponents say a final 'No', but you believe it is **still possible** to go on fighting. For example, if a zebra crossing is provided but without the lights, is it advisable to cut your losses, or should you go on fighting for lights to be added? This is difficult. If local people feel that a zebra crossing is still inadequate, then it might be worthwhile continuing to fight for lights. If the zebra crossing has improved safety enough to make further argument difficult, then give up trying to turn it into a pelican crossing. You can't win every battle but at least you tried.

How to decide

Ask yourself now:

- Have we **achieved** our objective?
- If we have not got what we wanted, is the result a **reasonable compromise?**
- Have we **failed** entirely to get what we wanted?
- Is there **scope for continuing** the campaign?
- Is there scope for **another campaign?**
- Is there **enough support** for a new campaign?

WHAT TO DO NEXT

There are certain things that must be done whether the campaign has been won or lost. Do them promptly and efficiently so that you are not being contacted for several months afterwards about things which should have been dealt with.

Informing supporters

It might be obvious to you that the campaign is over, but it might not be to other people. Take time to call a meeting. Let everyone discuss whether the end has come and, if so, how to wind everything up.

If a minority think that the campaign should go on and other people disagree, then it will be up to those who want to continue to start a new campaign. Any new group must, of course, have a new name and re-apply as a new group for any grant. It must ask for its own donations and provide its own publicity. To use the finances and name of the original group could cause legal difficulties for both groups.

If it is agreed that the campaign has finished, then a **letter of explanation** must go out to supporters. This could include thanks for their help, but it might be more sensible to wait a week to let people assimilate the announcement and then to send out the letter of thanks separately.

Thanks

Write out a list of *everybody* who has given you help or support during the campaign, and **thank them.** This is very important. Not only is it a vital courtesy, but you might want people's help for some other project of yours and you want them to think kindly of the campaign.

People to thank might include:

- supporters
- helpers
- committee members
- councillors
- MPs
- experts who have helped
- officers who have helped
- editors
- opponents who have been as helpful as they were allowed to be
- individuals who have given particularly helpful support.

It would be difficult to write a personal letter to large groups of people individually. In that case, use other means, such as:

- sending out a **leaflet** of thanks
- putting an **ad** in the local papers

SAVE MILL STREET PLAYGROUND CAMPAIGN

Mary Brown   Sheila Smith
7 Midfield Road   19 Barton Close
Fairfield   Fairfield

tel: Fairfield 1234   tel: Fairfield 5678

Dear Friend

On behalf of the campaign we are writing to thank you for
your loyal support during the past year. Without the efforts
of many people like yourself working together to benefit the
community, the campaign would not have had such an
impact. We are sure you are as pleased as we are that the
campaign was successful and that the playground has been
saved.

The campaign has now ended and to celebrate this we are
holding a party at Fairfield village hall on Friday 7th July at
7.00 p.m. Food will be provided but please bring a bottle!
We do hope you will be there to celebrate with us.

Yours faithfully

Mary Brown   Sheila Smith
Joint Chairwoman   Joint Chairwoman

A sample letter of thanks

- putting up **notices** of thanks in public places, such as libraries
- writing a short **article** of thanks for local papers, newsletters, and so on.

People who have given particular help or help over a long period must have an **individual** letter, signed by the chairman or the secretary. You may be able to deliver some of these by hand if you are short of money for the postage.

All these letters of thanks may take some time, but don't skip the job. Telephoning is not the same.

Informing the press

It is important to inform the press when the campaign is finished. If they have been giving you publicity during the time of the campaign, it is polite to let them know the outcome.

Of course, if the campaign is over because you have won, they will not want to be deprived of a possible celebratory article or photo!

Don't forget to include the **editors** in the list of those people to thank.

Records

In a fit of euphoria you might feel tempted to throw your collection of box files and papers relating to the campaign onto the nearest bonfire! Don't.

For a start it is wise to **keep the campaign papers** for at least six months, just in case anybody wants to see them or ask you questions about them. Perhaps someone has a spare cupboard where they could be kept for that time.

You might in the aftermath wish to write something about the events and need to refresh your memory from the files.

Financial records in particular must be kept for at least seven years so that if anyone wishes to see the books, or a grant-giving body asks about the finances, you have all the relevant papers to hand.

It might also be that someone starting a related campaign might find your papers useful as a guide to what might happen.

Money

One of the most important things you must do if you are sure the campaign is really over is to wind up the finances to the satisfaction of the campaign group.

As a first priority any **outstanding bills** for such things as printing or hire of halls must be paid.

Then, if you have been given a grant you will be expected to **pay back** any money which remains from that grant at the close of the cam-

SAVE MILL STREET PLAYGROUND CAMPAIGN

M. Brown
7 Midfield Road
Fairfield
tel: Fairfield 1234

S. Smith
19 Barton Close
Fairfield
tel: Fairfield 5678

PLAYGROUND SAVED!

THANK YOU
TO ALL SUPPORTERS
FROM
THE CAMPAIGN COMMITTEE

Printed by:
ABC Printers
12 Wild Place
Fairfield

Published by:
Save Mill Street
Playground Campaign
19 Barton Close
Fairfield

A leaflet of thanks

BUILD WHYTOWN SCHOOL CROSSING
MOVEMENT

The Committee thanks everyone for their support.
Sorry we didn't win. Campaign now ends.
J. Notts. tel: Whytown 91011

An ad in the local press at the end of a campaign

paign or at the end of the following financial year, whichever has been specified.

To do this the treasurer should ask the bank to close the campaign account and get a cheque for the outstanding sum made out to the grant-giving body. This must be sent to them. Remember to get a receipt for the records. A cheque for any petty cash remaining must also be sent where this has been taken out of grant money.

If after any outstanding grant money has been accounted for, there is any money remaining, perhaps from donations or subscriptions, the committee must decide what should be done with it. Work out the cost of final auditing, thank you letters, printing costs, typing costs, thank you leaflets, and so on. Then the rest should be **disposed of.** How to do this may be stated in your constitution. If it is kept in a bank account it will be forgotten and if kept in cash it will get lost or someone will be accused of spending it. For this reason it is unwise to keep a little 'on hand' in case it is needed. There is usually a rule in a constitution forbidding distribution of property to members.

Unless otherwise ruled, you could consider making a donation to an organisation with similar aims to the campaign, to a similar campaign in a different area, or to a completely unrelated but worthy cause that everyone agrees on.

Whatever you do with the remaining money, it must be **recorded** so that anyone can see that it was not spent on riotous living.

When closing the account ask for a **final statement** from the bank, and make sure as well that your **petty cash records** are up to date. Check that you have all the relevant **invoices** and **receipts.** Finally, send up-to-date accounts, invoices, receipts, and so on, audited if necessary, to the people who need to see them, such as groups who have supported you financially and want to see where their money went. Keep copies if the originals are needed.

EVALUATING THE CAMPAIGN

The group might feel it useful to compile a **record** of how the campaign went. This could be a source of helpful guidance if people wish to be involved in other campaigns. Such an evaluation could involve group discussion to work out what you did right and wrong.

Group discussion
The group could try:

● writing a list of things the campaign *did* right and wrong
● making a separate list of what the campaign *should have done*

● writing a short report to members based on these lists and keeping it on record.

Some questions you could ask as a basis for discussion are:

● Did you think the campaign was effective?
● If it was effective, what made it so?
● If the campaign was a failure, what mistakes were made?
● Was there enough support for the campaign?
● Were the finances adequate?
● Was the publicity handled well?

After such a group discussion John and his supporters concluded that their campaign for a pelican crossing failed because firstly they did not publicise it enough, and secondly they relied on donations from individuals and so did not have enough money.

Recording experiences
It is a good idea to encourage everyone to **write down** their own feelings and experiences about the campaign. Articles based on these reports could be offered to local newssheets or even the papers — the experiences recorded could be of help to others who are thinking of starting their own campaign.

Keep these notes with the other records for reference or for future publication.

AFTER IT'S OVER

Running a campaign, or taking an active part in one, is rather like drinking too much champagne. The high is wonderful, but you get a terrible feeling when it's all over.

People who run campaigns complain of the amount of time it takes, the strain, the worry, the cost, the sheer drudging effort of doing it. But they also love the feeling of being useful, of doing something worthwhile, of being in charge. And if they get publicity, well, how exciting it all is.

But at whatever level you are involved, when the campaign is over you will feel let down. The adrenalin that kept you going has stopped flowing, and exhaustion sets in. What should you do?

Throw a party
This is not as crazy as it sounds. What better way to mark the end of a campaign, either to say 'well done and thank you' to your supporters, or 'let's congratulate ourselves for giving it a good try'? It needn't cost much. Make it a 'bring a bottle' or 'bring your own food' party. Invite

all your helpers — and even your opponents. It will make the end seem as important as the beginning.

Write it down
Even if you only do so for your own interest, it will get it out of your system. You might even want to interest other people in publishing some of your thoughts.

Start another campaign
Be careful about this one. Why are you doing it? Is it just because you miss the excitement of the last campaign or do you really care about the new cause? Take some time out of campaigning first to give yourself a new perspective. At least if you start again you'll know what you are letting yourself in for.

Whatever you decide to do, you can feel a **sense of satisfaction.** You did your best for your **local community** and nobody can do more than that.

Chapter checklist
● When you have achieved your original objective, stop the campaign.
● If you think more than your original objective could be achieved, consider a separate campaign.
● Make sure all your supporters understand why the campaign has ended, especially if the result is inconclusive.
● Make sure you thank all your supporters, and notify the press.
● Be careful to wind up the finances properly, and return any unused grant.
● Keep complete records for 6 months after the end in case you need to refer to them again. Keep financial records for 7 years.
● Evaluate the campaign and keep a record of your findings as an aid to future campaigners.

A Sample Grant Application Form

This application form is reproduced with the permission of Southwark Women's Equality Unit.

LONDON BOROUGH OF SOUTHWARK
ONE-OFF GRANT APPLICATION FORM

Ref. No.	Date Received	Committee
. . . .	. . . .	. . . .

This form will be photocopied, please type or print in BLACK ink.

PLEASE READ THE GUIDANCE NOTES CAREFULLY BEFORE COMPLETING THIS FORM.

1. Name of Organisation ....
....

2. Address of Organisation ....
....

3. Name and address of contact person ....
....

Position in organisation ....

4. Telephone: Day .... Evening ....

5. When was your organisation formed? ....

6. (a) Is your organisation a registered charity?   YES/NO

   If YES, please state your registration no. ....

   (b) Is your organisation a Limited Company? YES/NO

7. Please state:

    (a) Name of Bank ....

    (b) Address of Bank ....

    ....

    (c) Bank Account Name ....

    (d) Bank Account No. ....

8. Do you have a constitution?   YES/NO

    If YES, please attach a copy to the application, unless one has already been sent in with another application.

9. Describe the aims and objectives of your organisation and the needs it seeks to meet.

10. Give an estimate of the number of people who make use/will use your activities.

    ....

11. Which part of the borough do your activities cover? (eg ward, borough-wide).

    ....

12. What percentage of your users live in the borough?

    ....

    If none, please say why ....

    ....

    ....

13. Do you employ staff?   YES/NO

    If YES, please give numbers, positions and grades.

14. **Your Organisation's Commitment to Equal Opportunities**
    The Council has an Equal Opportunities Policy, which states that it is actively opposed to racism, sexism and all forms of discrimina-

tion faced by black people and other ethnic minorities. The Council is seeking to implement a programme of positive action to make this policy fully effective.

In line with this the Council expects all grant aided organisations to have an equal opportunities policy.

(a) Does your Organisation have an Equal Opportunities Policy?

YES/NO

If YES, please attach a copy of your Equal Opportunities Policy/Statement.

(b) Please give the percentage breakdown as per the following:—

	Women	Black people and other Ethnic Minority	People with Disabilities
i) Users			
ii) Staff			
iii) Management Committee			

15. Where do the group activities take place? ....
....

(a) Do these premises have access and facilities for people with disabilities? Please specify
....
....

16. (a) Please state the total amount of grant you are applying for:—

£...........

(b) Please state why you need the grant.

....
....
....

17. Please give a breakdown of costs of the grant you are applying for.

ITEM	COST
	£
TOTAL	£

18. *The Organisation's present finances:*
Please enclose a copy of your organisation's latest accounts and income and expenditure statement OR if not available fill in the following:

(a)   RECURRING REVENUE EXPENDITURE

1. Staff Costs   Full Year's Costs
— No. of Full-time Staff .... Total Salary Cost .... £
— No. of Part-time Staff .... Total Salary Cost .... £

2. Administration eg.
— Postage   £
— Stationery   £
— Office equipment   £
— Printing and Publicity   £
— Telephone Bills   £
— Other (please specify)   £

3. Overheads eg.
— Rent   £
— Rates   £
— Other (please specify)   £

                      Total Expenditure   £

INCOME USED FOR REVENUE EXPENDITURE

                                                   Full Year

1. Grant Aid
— Greater London Arts Association   £
— London Borough Grants Scheme   £

— London Borough of Southwark   £
— Urban Programme   £
— ILEA   £
— Other Boroughs (please specify)   £
— Commercial/Industrial Sponsorship   £
— Trusts   £
— Other (please specify)   £

2. Earned Income
— Fund Raising Events   £
— Membership Fees   £
— Charges to Users   £
— Other (please specify)   £

                        Total Income   £

(b)   CAPITAL
    Expenditure   Full Year's Cost (£)
— Acquisition of buildings   £
— Construction or renovation costs   £
— Feasibility Study   £
— Other Professional Fees   £
— Equipment and furniture   £
— Other costs (Please specify)   £

                        Total Expenditure £

    Income used for Capital Expenditure
— London Borough Grants Scheme   £
— London Borough of Southwark   £
— Urban Programme   £
— ILEA   £
— Other Boroughs (please specify)   £
— Commercial/Industrial Sponsorship   £
— Trusts   £
— Other (please specify)   £

                        Total Income   £

19. Have you applied to any other funding bodies for the same grant
    being requested for in this application?   YES/NO.

    If YES, please give details

20. Do any Council Officers know about your organisation? YES/NO

    If YES please give the following details:

    Name ....

    Telephone No. (if known) ....

    Department (if known) ....

21. Please fill in the attached Appendix.

22. To the best of my knowledge, the information included in this form is correct. I have read and agree to abide by the Council's Conditions of Grant Aid if my application is successful.

    Name of Organisation ....

    Signed ....

    Date ....

    Position in Organisation ....

23. Please remember to include with this Form (if applicable)
    1. Constitution
    2. Equal opportunities policy/statement
    3. Names and addresses of Management Group
    4. Last Year's accounts or financial records
    5. Any other supportive material

Please complete the following table as accurately as you can.

This will enable us to decide on the legal powers the Council can use to award the grant to your organisation.

NAME OF ORGANISATION ....

Below is a list of activities (a-q) some of which your organisation will provide.

Please: i) tick those your group provides
                  and
           ii) estimate, out of 100, what proportion
               each one is of all your activities.

		Please tick	Percentage %
(a)	Providing recreational and/or social activities and/or sports activities		
(b)	Providing arts and crafts activities		
(c)	Providing entertainments, music and/or dancing activities		
(d)	Providing cultural activities		
(e)	Providing information about local government services or matters and/or government department services and/or services provided by any voluntary organisation or charity (including yourself)		
(f)	Investigating and/or collecting information on any matters concerning Greater London or any part of it and/or publishing such information		
(g)	Providing information on tenants' rights		

	Please tick	Percentage %
(h) Any matters relating to homelessness (including advice)		
(i) Providing advice to consumers of goods or services in Southwark		
(j) Providing facilities for exhibitions or conferences		
(k) Providing library services to the public		
(l) Making provision for care of children under 5		
(m) Providing transport for the disabled		
(n) Promoting welfare of the disabled other than (m) above		
(o) Promoting welfare of the elderly		
(p) Promoting care of the sick and/or the prevention of illness (including providing advice on where to obtain treatment)		
(q) Other (please give as much detail as you can)		
	TOTAL	100%

Glossary

AEI (Adult Education Institute) A centre for adult learning.

AGM (Annual General Meeting) Yearly meeting of an organisation at which officers are elected and accounts approved.

Artwork A line illustration or photograph suitable for reproduction by a printer.

Census An official count of inhabitants, taken every 10 years, and statistics relating to it.

CHC (Community Health Council) Organisation which monitors the actions of the health authority in its area.

Constituency A division of an area for voting purposes. It is represented in Parliament by an MP.

Constitution A set of rules for governing an organisation.

Copy Matter for printing.

Copy date/Deadline Latest time by which an editor must receive copy so that it can be printed.

Dot-matrix Material produced by a computer which is printed by an arrangement of dots.

Fly posting Illegally sticking up posters in public places.

Invoice Bill for goods or services supplied on credit.

Logo Design used to represent an organisation.

Management Committee The ruling committee of a group or groups.

Minutes Written summary providing an accurate record of which happened at a meeting.

Mole Person who provides people outside his organisation with material which is not meant to be seen by the public.

Motion A formal proposal, requiring a decision, put before a meeting.

Petition A written request to authority signed by many people.

Press release Written statement to the press.

PRO (Public Relations Officer) Person in charge of organising publicity for, and providing information about, an organisation.

Quorum Minimum number of people who must be present at a meeting before any business can be conducted.

Standing orders Permanent rules for conducting a meeting.

Surgery A regular advice session held by a councillor or MP for his constituents.

Ward An administrative division of a constituency which is represented by councillors.

Useful Addresses

Able-Label, Steepleprint Ltd, Northampton NN6 0LS (tel: 0604-810781).

Asian Herald, Room 23/24, Wickham House, 10 Cleveland Way, London E1 4TR (tel: 01-790 2424).

Asian Times, Tower House, 139-149 Fonthill Road, Finsbury Park, London N4 3HF (tel: 01-281 1191).

Association of Free Newspapers, Ladybellgate House, Longsmith Street, Gloucester GL1 2HT (tel: 0452-26561).

The British Insurance Brokers Association, Biba House, 14 Bevis Marks, London EC3A 7NT (tel: 01-623 9043).

Caribbean Times, Tower House, 139-149 Fonthill Road, Finsbury Park, London N4 3HF (tel: 01-281 1191).

Community Information Project, 136 City Road, London EC1V 2NJ (tel: 01-251 8616).

Conservative & Unionist Party, 32 Smith Square, London SW1P 3HH (tel: 01-222 9000).

Directory of Social Change, 9 Mansfield Place, London NW3.

The Ecology Party, 36-38 Clapham Road, London SW9 (tel: 01-735 2485).

The Gleaner, Ventura House, 176-188 Acre Lane, London SW2 5UL (tel: 01-733 7014).

The Green Party, 10 Station Parade, Balham High Road, London SW12 (tel: 01-673 0045).

House of Commons, Westminster, London SW1A 0AA (tel: 01-219 3000).

The Institute of Chartered Accountants in England & Wales (ICAEW), PO Box 433, Chartered Accountants Hall, Moorgate Place, London EC2P 2BJ (tel: 01-628 7060).

The Labour Party, 150 Walworth Road, London SE17 1JT (tel: 01-703 0833).

Law Centres Federation, Duchess House, 18-19 Warren Street, London W1P 5DB (tel: 01-387 8570).

Magnum Shirts, Rose House, Dunsfold Road, Loxhill, Godalming, Surrey GU8 4BJ (tel: (Hascombe) 048632-481).

National Association of Citizens' Advice Bureaux, Myddleton House, 115/123 Pentonville Road, London N1 9LZ (tel: 01-833 2181).

National Council for Civil Liberties, 21 Tabard Street, London SE1 4LA (tel: 01-403 3888).

National Council for Voluntary Organisations, 26 Bedford Square, London WC1B 3HU (tel: 01-636 4066).

National Federation of Community Organisations, 8-9 Upper Street, London N1 0PQ (tel: 01-226 0189).

New Life, 8-16 Coronet Street, Off Old Street, London N1 6HD (tel: 01-729 5453).

New Voice, 122 Seventh Avenue, Manor Park, London E12 5JH.

Plaid Cymru, 51 Cathedral Road, Cardiff CF1 9HD (tel: 0222-31944).

Registrar of Companies, Company Registration Office (CRO), Crown House, Crown Way, Maindy, Cardiff CF4 3UZ (tel: 0222-388588), 102 George Street, Edinburgh EH2 3DJ, IDB House, 64 Chichester Street, Belfast BT1 4JX.

SAVE Britain's Heritage, 68 Battersea High Street, London Sw11 3BX (tel: 01-228 3336).

Scottish Council for Voluntary Organisations, 18-19 Claremont Crescent, Edinburgh EH7 4QD (tel: 031-556 3882).

Scottish National Party, 6 North Charlotte Street, Edinburgh EH2 4JH (tel: 031-226 3661).

Services for Community Action & Tenants, 15 Micawber Street, London N1 7TB (tel: 01-253 3627) *and* 31 Brook Road, Sheffield S8 9FH (tel: 0742-550010).

Social & Liberal Democrats, 4 Cowley Street, London SW1P 3NB (tel: 01-222 7999).

Sussex T-Shirt Co, River Road, Littlehampton, W. Sussex BN17 5BZ (tel: 0903-717298 & 723843).

Trades Union Congress (TUC), Congress House, Great Russell Street, London WC1B 3LS (tel: 01-636 4030).

Universal Button Co Ltd, 1-9 Birbeck Street, Bethnal Green, London E2 6JZ (tel: 01-739 5750 & 8309).

The Voice, 94 Bow Road, London E3 3AA (tel: 01-980 4444).

The Volunteer Centre, 29 Lower King's Road, Berkhamsted, Herts HP4 2AB (tel: 04427-7331).

Wales Council for Voluntary Action, Llys Ifor, Crescent Road, Caeffili CF8 1XL (tel: 869224/869111).

West Indian News, 379-381 Brixton Road, London SW9 7DE (tel: 01-733 7052).

Further Reading

The Alternative Printing Handbook, Chris Treweek & Jonathan Zeitlyn (Penguin, 1983)

A-Z of Britain's Free Newspapers & Magazines (Association of Free Newspapers)

The A-Z of Finding Out, Robert Walker (Pan, 1983)

Citizen Action: Taking Action in Your Local Community, Des Wilson (Longman, 1986)

Citrine's ABC of Chairmanship, Eds: Michael Cannell & Norman Citrine (NCLC Publishing Society Ltd, 1982)

The Community Organisations Survival Kit (National Federation of Community Organisations, 1982)

Directory of Grant Making Trusts (Charities Aid Foundation, 1985)

Do-It-Yourself Graphic Design, Ed: John Laing (Ebury Press, 1984)

Face the Press: A Practical Guide to Press & Public Relations for the Smaller Organisations, James Hodge (Management Update, 1986)

Fundraising: A Comprehensive Handbook, Hilary Blume (Routledge & Kegan Paul, 1977)

Guide to the Major Grant Making Trusts, Ed: Luke FitzHerbert and Michael Eastwood (Directory of Social Change, annually)

Holding Your Ground: An Action Guide to Local Conservation, Angela King & Sue Clifford (Maurice Temple Smith)

How to Do Your Own Advertising Michael Bennie (Northcote House, 1989)

How to Keep Business Accounts, Peter Taylor (Northcote House, 1988)

How to Manage Your Money, If You Have Any: An Accountancy Handbook for Community Organisations (The Community Accountancy Project, available through National Federation of Community Organisations, 1983)

Manual for Action, Martin Jelfs (Action Resource Group, 1982)

Organising Things: A Guide to Successful Political Action, Sue Ward (Pluto Press, 1982)

The Penguin Guide to Law, John Pritchard (Penguin, 2nd Edition, 1988)

Pressure: The A-Z of Campaigning in Britain, Des Wilson (Heinemann, 1984)

Self-Help Groups: Getting Started, Keeping Going, Judy Wilson (Longman, 1986)

Using the Media, Denis MacShane (Pluto Press, 1979)

Voluntary but not Amateur: A guide to the law for voluntary organisations and community groups, Duncan Forbes, Ruth Hayes & Jacki Reason (London Voluntary Service Council, 1988)

Voluntary Organisations & The Media, Maggie Jones (Bedford Square Press, 1984)

Who Decides What: The Citizens' Handbook, Klaus Boehm & Brian Morris (Macmillan, 1979)

Willings Press Guide (British Media Publications, annually)

Writers' & Artists' Yearbook (A & C Black, annually)

Index